MW01252708

Walking
The Keys
To Happiness

Practical advice and humorous memories from a week long walk of The Florida Keys

Tamara Scharf

www.walkingthekeys.com

www.tamarascharf.com

Copyright © 2016 by Tamara Scharf

Disclaimer

The Information provided within this book is for general informational purposes only. Every effort has been made to make this book as accurate as possible.

However, there may be topographical and/or content errors. Therefore, this book should serve only as a general guide and not as the ultimate source of subject information.

This book is not intended to provide advice and guidance on which the readers can rely and is not intended to encourage readers to engage in a particular activity.

The information contained within this book is for educational purposes only. If the reader wishes to apply ideas contained in this book, the reader is taking full responsibility for his/her actions.

Readers must not rely on the information in this book as an alternative to legal or medical advice from an appropriately qualified individual.

This book is not intended to be a substitute for the medical advice of a licensed physician. Before embarking on a new exercise program or a strenuous walk as described in this book, the reader should consult with their doctor.

The author and publisher shall have no liability or responsibility to any person or entity regarding any loss or damage incurred, directly or indirectly, by the information contained in this book.

The greatest heroines are songs unsung:

Let the joyous news be spread

Tamara Scharf The Keys did tread

Battling heat, pain and bites

She onward trudged and slept by nights

A record-breaking walk she completed

Now where's the love for this undefeated?

Raise your glass, or two, or three

Cause no one is more impressed than me

(and a thousand others)

Annie Greer

Contents

Introduction

What you are holding in your hand is the result of a "last hurrah" idea. I was getting ready to leave Florida but decided I wasn't going to go without a last adventure. Born and bred in Germany, I have always been somewhat of an adventurer. I have lived, studied and worked in various places on two continents. This included a long spell of almost seventeen happy years in the United Kingdom and the Channel Islands. I spent a decade living and working on the beautiful island of Guernsey, which is roughly twenty-four square miles small. After over ten years on this little island, I got itchy feet and made a bid for freedom when my place of work closed its doors. Having no family of my own and no dependents, I decided to travel and work on cruise ships in a warmer climate. After various deviations, this decision eventually landed me in sunny Florida.

In the weeks leading up to my "last hurrah", I was very much down on my luck. I had been witness to a crime which shook me, and lost my job shortly after. For those reasons and others, I had decided it was finally time to bite the bullet and return to Europe, even though I did not really want to go back. I had no plan, no idea and no motivation. I was pretty much down in the dumps, not to say depressed, for weeks. I had lost my ability to think positively and felt stuck. On top of it all, I did not want to leave my condo by the ocean without a satisfactory alternative to look forward to.

I decided to set myself a mental and physical challenge, to get away for a few days and push myself out of the comfort zone and this rut I was in. I wanted to prove to myself that I could achieve something a little extraordinary. I hoped to gain inspiration, motivation and energy for the next stage of my life. Last but not least, I wanted to adequately celebrate my time in sunny Florida and leave on a positive note, rather than feel miserable and depressed. I did have some wonderful times and made some great friends. In order to celebrate the good times, there had to be a "last hurrah". The decision was made in October 2013: I will walk the entire Florida Keys solo!

Why Walk? I have always loved how walking, especially in nature, stimulates the mind and refreshes ones outlook on life. Walks have often been my escape and my "happy place". I always returned physically tired from my walks, but mentally refreshed and with new energy. As well as the usual smaller walks and strolls, for the last few years I particularly liked to embark on more strenuous all day walks, steadily increasing length and distance. Previously, I had walked for no more than two consecutive days - a weekend by myself in a hilly and wooded area in Germany. Attempting to walk The Florida Keys in one week was to be my longest walk so far.

Why The Florida Keys? My thought process leading up to the decision to walk The Keys in particular, was quite simple: it's a safe route with no chance of getting lost, it will be warm so I don't need to take much "stuff", and I love The Keys, so walking them would be fun. The decision was quickly made.

I wrote this book for two main reasons. Firstly, there was the wish to provide some inspiration to anyone who is planning a little (or big) adventure of this kind. I want to inspire and say: don't put it off for later, just get out there. It really isn't that difficult or taxing. Don't be discouraged because you don't consider yourself fit enough, young enough or brave enough to do it alone. You don't have to be a world-class athlete, run marathons or walk 2000 miles to feel a sense of achievement and pride. Going for a walk, short or long distance, is as simple as putting one foot in front of the other. Fact is: any challenge that pushes us out of our comfort zone can do wonders for self-esteem and help gain a new perspective on life. It certainly helped me.

My other reason for writing this book was having a bunch of funny material in form of journal entries from the walk. My journal not only contains the day by day account of the walk from Key Largo to Key West, but also illustrates the quirkiness and loveliness of The Florida Keys and their people. Of course, it also contains plenty of evidence as to my naivety at the start of the walk, my resourcefulness and the resolve not to give up (even when in pain). There is plenty of reference to my daily aches and pains, as well as all the funny, interesting and unusual things and people I came across. This is interspersed with a little history here and there. It seemed a waste to lock the journal away somewhere gathering dust. Although I'll let you be the judge of that.

The book contains two somewhat separate parts. The first part gives the reader a general overview of the benefits, history and reasons for multi-day walks, as well as advice on how to plan such a walk. This part contains the results of my quest and research for information whilst preparing for the walk, plus some of the experience collected en route through the Florida Keys. It includes suggestions on equipment, packing and how to structure walking days. Most - if not all - of my suggestions can be applied to similar length walks in a warm or mild climate.

The second part of the book is largely about my own and very personal experience, starting with the planning of the walk and the arrival in Key Largo on the Greyhound Bus. It includes a day by day account of the walk to my final destination - Mile Marker 0 in Key West - as well as plenty of references to the history of the Florida Keys and suggestions of "things to do".

This part of the book also contains my somewhat humorous personal journal entries from the walk, so it might benefit from being read with an open mind, not least as it contains a little adult material. Don't say I didn't warn you. At the very least, I hope to not only to provide my readers with a couple of hours of light entertainment, but also a good chuckle here and there at my expense.

CHAPTER 1

Why Walk When You Can Drive?

Why walk when you can drive? What a great question. Being an avid walker, I get asked this question all the time. I am now pretty practiced at answering it. There are some very good reasons to walk "when you can drive", some of which I have outlined below.

1. The Benefits Of Walking For The Body

I was introduced to regular outdoor exercise from a very young age and vividly remember going for daily walks with my grandmother through fields, meadows and woods. Perhaps this explains why I have always loved exercise and especially walking. Luckily, it is possible to walk pretty much anywhere with no cost and in almost any weather. All one needs is the right clothing, footwear and resolve. Having lived in the UK for seventeen years, I managed to do a lot of walking despite the ubiquitous rain and wind.

According to the American Heart Association (www.heart.org), there are considerable benefits of walking for the body. As little as thirty minutes per day of moderate walking can achieve the following benefits:

- Reduction in the risk of coronary heart disease.
- Improvement of blood pressure and blood sugar levels.

- Improvement of blood lipid profile.
- Maintaining body weight and lowering the risk of obesity.
- Reducing the risk of osteoporosis.
- Reducing the risk of breast and colon cancer.
- Reducing the risk of non-insulin dependent (type 2) diabetes.

Of course, walking is also great for muscles, helping to tone up particularly leg muscles, with comparatively little effort and low impact on joints. Walking gets fresh air into our lungs and as a by-product of walking outside, our body produces Vitamin D from the sunrays we soak up in nature. Walking in nature, therefore, should make us feel virtuous about the good things we are doing for our body.

2. The Benefits Of Walking For The Mind

Apparently, "nature experience reduces rumination and subgenual prefrontal cortex activation", according to recent research (www.pnas.org). Sounds intriguing, but what does this mean in lay terms? In short, it means walking in nature makes us sulk less and calms down our brains, both of which allegedly reduce our risk of going crazy.

It is not my intention to make light of mental illness at all, but having succumbed to the odd bout of depression in the past, I can personally attest to walking being beneficial for my state of mind. Walking in nature indeed helps lift my spirits, makes me feel more alert, more positive and function better all around. I found beach walks particularly effective and calming for the mind, helping me to "ruminate" less about negative events and thoughts, as well as getting oxygen into my body and brain, helping to blow away those cobwebs.

Apparently, walking also slows down ageing. There have been a few studies on how exercise, and particularly walking, affects the part of the brain responsible for memory. In a controlled study on the walking-brain-memory connection in older adults, walking has actually been proven to slow down the effects of aging on the mind (Susan Krauss Whitbourne PhD in "Psychology Today", Feb 2011).

It seems the experts have concluded that our brains will thank us for every step we take.

3. Walking For Spiritual Reasons

Humans have walked for spiritual and religious reasons for hundreds and possibly thousands of years across all religions: Jews walk to Jerusalem, Christians go to the Holy Land and Muslims make the journey to Mecca.

The traditional reason for embarking on a pilgrimage was (and still is in some cultures) to search penance of one's sins. Most commonly, a pilgrimage in former centuries could be as short as just a few miles to a local Saint's tomb or shrine. A longer pilgrimage might be as long as many hundreds of miles, such as the Camino de Santiago in Spain, once a very popular pilgrimage for Christians all over Europe. The Camino has seen a marked rise in popularity again over recent years.

Increasingly, in this day and age, people elect to go on short or longer "pilgrimages" without wanting to attribute any religious significance to their walks. Rather, the modern day pilgrimages are often carried out for contemplative and spiritual reasons. Pilgrimages and long walks over several days or even weeks can be inspiring, contemplative, challenging and of course fun. They can take one away from modern day stresses, responsibilities and worries, and have the potential to be life-changing. One might go on a long walk to "find oneself", perhaps after an illness or a job loss or even a bereavement.

The reasons for a pilgrimage can be many, not necessarily originating from a negative event. Sometimes, the reasons for a long walk can be the wish of setting oneself a challenge, wanting to be alone in nature for contemplation, or simply to train the body and shape up. Some might also decide to embark on a long walk for fundraising to support a charity or another worthwhile cause.

While every person will have their unique reason or several reasons for a modern-day pilgrimage, the benefits hold true for all: walking over several days is a great way to get back to ones spiritual essence and realign with nature. A multi-day walk provides us with a temporary retreat away from modern civilization with all its hustle, bustle and distractions.

4. My Personal Reasons For Walking

I have to confess: I am neither religious nor overly spiritually inclined. I am pragmatic and walk when I feel like it, which happens to be almost every day. Walking for most of my errands too, I see it as a practical way to keep fit in every day life, without trying too hard. It has the welcome side-effects of reducing my carbon footprint and reducing money spent on fuel or public transport.

Most of all, I love the quiet contemplation that comes with a walk in nature and being alone with one's thoughts, feelings and surroundings. I love putting one step in front of the other, a seemingly small feat that by the end of the day often served to transport me over quite a distance. Once I get going, I will often walk for many miles.

I love all the nature, people and animals I might see and meet along the way. I immensely enjoy everything passing me by in "slow motion" and when I see something beautiful or interesting, it is easy to slow down and stop. This is pretty much impossible when driving, having to keep our eyes firmly on the road and traffic. The beauty of everyday life and nature is mostly passing us by and we might even get aggravated by traffic and inconsiderate drivers. Walking is the antidote to sitting in a metal box with four wheels and racing from A to B as fast as possible, all the while concentrating on the road and not being able to appreciate our surroundings.

I certainly believe in walking being a key to happiness. Walking is almost a miracle cure and as we have seen, it can help us to ruminate less, keep our bodies healthy and our minds active and happy. Having walked myself out of quite a few crises in my life, I am living proof: it works!

CHAPTER 2

Why walk The Florida Keys?

We have just established that walking is good for us and lifts our spirits, but that doesn't mean we have to walk 105 long miles in less than a week in a hot environment, right?

Well, yes and no.

There are obviously those who do believe driving is better than walking in some instances. In my case, I wanted to walk for enjoyment and in order to see the wonderful ocean views that this particular route – The Florida Keys – would hold in store.

However, there was undoubtedly another big reason for me to attempt a longer and time-pressured walk as opposed to just an hour's worth of a Sunday stroll: the physical and mental challenge.

I had been going through some personal issues, such as a run-in with a criminal and, later on, losing a job. I had been more or less permanently single for a number of years and didn't really have much luck in dating either. All in all, I felt pretty dispirited and down, and needed to get out of the "I feel sorry for myself" rut. I desperately needed to re-connect with myself and nature. I wanted to set a feasible challenge that wasn't too big to achieve, and one that I could do alone and unaided. I wanted to test the limits of my body strength as well as my psychological strength, hence the idea for the walk was born. Below are some of the main reasons why I picked The Florida Keys in particular and why I recommend walking them.

5. A Little About The Florida Keys

The Florida Keys are an archipelago of coral reef origin, and begin at the southeastern tip of the Florida peninsula mainland, about fifteen miles south of Miami. The Keys (from the Spanish "Cayo" for "Island") form an arc of many small islands. This arc of islands and submerged reefs can be tracked south-southwest all the way down to Key West, the westernmost of the inhabited islands, and on to the uninhabited Dry Tortugas.

The Florida Keys were found and charted by Juan Ponce de Leon in 1513. Only accessible by water until the early 20th century, however, they remained sparsely populated until fairly recent times, with one notable exception: Key West.

Key West already had a population of 18.000 souls in the mid-1800s, making it the largest city in Florida. While Key West was thriving on the wrecking industry, The Florida Keys in general remained difficult to populate until fairly recently due to their somewhat remote location, mosquito plagues and the relative lack of ways to make a good living.

A marked change occurring in the early 20th century can mostly be attributed to the extension of Henry Flagler's Florida East Coast Railway (FECR). The arrival of the railroad revolutionized transport to the Florida Keys and preceded a rise in population and a better infrastructure for the island chain. Nowadays, the population of The

Florida Keys is around 77.000, according to Monroe County's figures from the 2014 census (https://en.wikipedia.org/wiki/Monroe_County). Most of the population is concentrated in a few population-dense areas. Key West accounts for more than thirty percent of the entire population of The Keys with just under 26.000 inhabitants, according to the 2014 census figures.

The Florida Keys are of course easily accessible these days via US1, which is referred to as the "Overseas Highway". We owe the enjoyment of a most pleasant drive (or walk) mostly to Henry Flagler and his FECR extension to Key West, which was completed in 1912. At the time of construction, he was mocked a great deal for his "outrageous" vision and plan to build a railroad south of Miami, over some very large stretches of water. It is true that construction of the railroad extension into The Florida Keys came with a lot of setbacks and even loss of life. It had also acquired the less than flattering nickname "Flagler's Folly".

We must not forget that before Flagler embarked on this huge and daring project, which turned out to be anything but a folly, most of The Keys could only be reached by boat. Sadly, Flagler's railroad was relatively short lived. The Florida East Coast Railway extension was more or less abandoned in 1935, after large parts of it were destroyed in the devastating Labor Day Hurricane of that year.

Flagler's railroad arguably remains the number one reason for the extensive modern settlement of The Florida Keys. The Overseas Highway, to date the only road in and out of The Florida Keys, was practically built on what remained of Flagler's railroad and its bridges, many of which were converted to allow for vehicular traffic in the late 1930s.

To this day we either walk directly on stretches of road that were once railway line, or right next to the old railway bridges which, although now in disrepair, are still standing in some parts of the islands. I am particularly referring to the old 7 Mile Bridge and the old Bahia Honda Bridge. Both of these bridges are incredible engineering marvels. They are almost defiantly still standing and reminding us of a bygone era, despite getting a constant bashing from the elements.

One of the reasons for me to walk this particular route, therefore, was my interest in all things historic. I wanted to walk every step of the last part of US1 down to Mile Marker 0, to see the Overseas Highway and its many bridges in its entirety at my own pace. I wanted to pay homage to Flagler's vision and fortitude, having financed this entire project privately, never wavering despite being the target of many unkind jokes back in his day.

6. The Climate Of The Florida Keys

The climate of The Florida Keys is tropical with wet summers and drier winters, as is to be expected, with the southern tip of Key West a mere ninety miles distance from Cuba and the Caribbean. The Florida Keys are officially classified as a tropical savanna (according to the "Koeppen Climate Classification"). What does this mean for anybody who wants to attempt a walk of The Florida Keys? It's very good news for walkers who like it hot or at least warm and mild.

A tropical savanna is typically characterized by a very mild climate, and a wet and dry season. Little precipitation should be expected during the dry season, making the weather relatively predictable during that time of year. The dry season, roughly from November to April, is extremely pleasant in The Florida Keys with mild temperatures, little rainfall and usually a nice, sometimes stiff, breeze. As far as I am aware, there have been no recordings of frost anywhere from Key Largo down to Key West in the history of weather records. Sounds wonderful, doesn't it?

Of course, the warm climate played a huge role in my decision to walk The Florida Keys. I pictured myself listening to faint sounds of Jimmy Buffet songs "wasting awaaaay again in Margaritaville...la la la" coming from tiki bars along the way, while I would blissfully and effortlessly skip along US1. Perhaps I could even wear a bikini and a floppy hat? Plus, surely there would be rewards in form of delicious seafood, and drinks decorated with little colorful umbrellas, awaiting me at the end of the walking days.

Just as well I didn't know the reality back in the planning stage: the first and well deserved celebratory umbrella drink I got to taste was upon arrival and completion of my walk in Key West. Skipping along US1 wearing a bikini? I started off in shorts and T-shirt but in order to shelter from mosquitos and sun, I was longing for a full body hazmat suit from day 2 onwards.

I would certainly never recommend walking any length of The Florida Keys in summertime. The heat and humidity is exhausting and tough for the cardiovascular system in the summer months anywhere in South Florida. Additionally, the weather gets quite unpredictable with frequent afternoon storms that can appear from seemingly out of nowhere, in fact, you can watch the clouds grow to threatening thunderheads within minutes.

To put it descriptively: I would not want to be stuck in the middle of the 7 Mile Bridge in a roaring thunder storm with lightning all around me and cars speeding by. I hope this is sufficient warning to discourage anyone who might be tempted to walk The Keys in summertime, which roughly encompasses the months of June to September. If this isn't enough to put you off, consider this: in Florida, statistically speaking, you are more likely to get hit by a lightning strike (especially in the summer) than win the lottery. Enough said.

The logical time-frame to embark on a walk of The Florida Keys is any time from November to April. During this time, little rainfall is to be expected and the average daytime highs are around 75-80 degrees with lower humidity, according to the Key West Tourist Authority average temperature chart (http://www.fla-keys.com).

I personally chose the end of October for various reasons, some of which were based on personal circumstances, others on practicality. November until April happens to be the main tourist season in The Florida Keys, and I wanted to walk most of the route before the roads would become too busy and accommodation would not only get scarce but also much more expensive.

Winter is, after all, that time of year when the migratory snowbirds arrive on South Florida's shores. If you are not from Florida and don't know what snowbirds are, you might be forgiven for wondering why I am talking of a flock of migratory birds and why they would have an effect on accommodations and roads.

Let me explain: South Florida's human migratory birds come in cars from Canada, New York and other similarly ghastly cold and miserable places, when their home countries and home states have become too ghastly cold and miserable to stay there. The snowbirds then pack their bikinis and bathing shorts ("speedos" actually), jump into their cars and arrive here looking for some warm Florida sun, tiki bars and funnily enough: umbrella drinks.

The snowbirds are not always popular with the locals. Allegedly, many of them, when driving, seem to forget where their acceleration pedal is situated, possibly a direct result of indulging in too many of those umbrella drinks. Thus, the snowbirds are often accused of bringing traffic to a standstill, clogging up roads, (over-) populating tiki bars, restaurants and hotels, so much so that everywhere becomes crowded and expensive. This has of course done wonders for the economy, but that's a fact easily forgotten when the car with Quebec license plate drives at 40mph in front of you on the highway.

This whole migration business starts in October and gets into full swing by the holiday season. Therefore, walking The Florida Keys in wintertime and especially around the holidays, means you will get caught up in the flock, so be warned.

I digress. Let's get back to the climate. Of course, the weather is also advantageous in The Keys when it comes to the amount of gear and clothing to take for a multi-day walk. As it is always warm here, bar the odd day in wintertime when it might get to lower than 70 degrees temporarily, the amount of clothing needed can be kept to a bare minimum (no pun intended). This means one does not need to take more than a few changes of lightweight clothes such as T-shirts and shorts. It is prudent to include a sweater and water-proof windbreaker/poncho, just in case a cloud or front happens to forget that we are in dry season. Another major benefit of walking The Florida Keys is therefore: no added weight in form of warm or bulky clothing needed. Ever.

7. The Unimaginable Natural Beauty Of The Florida Keys

Here we have probably the number one reason why a walk of the entire Florida Keys island chain is such a life-enhancing and exhilarating adventure: the unbelievable and unimaginable natural beauty you will encounter at almost every step.

Yes, there are tiny little stretches where you will pound the pavement feeling less than enamored, like in any other place, past noisy traffic and in less manicured neighborhoods. Most of the time, however, you will be within just a few feet of the ocean (make that two oceans) with plenty of lovely properties, boats, greenery and wildlife to look at. The water is turquoise and inviting every step of the way and there is plenty of life to see in and out of the water.

Walking south, towards Key West, the vast Atlantic will accompany you on your left hand side all the way to Key West. On your right, you will see the wonderful and often mirror-calm waters of the Gulf of Mexico. The Overseas Highway leads across many bridges where the two oceans intermingle and it is possible to see plenty of fish in the currents. You will also notice that the locals do not talk about the Atlantic and the Gulf of Mexico, but refer to locations as being either "oceanside" (Atlantic) or "bayside" (Gulf of Mexico).

Frequently, the Overseas Highway borders almost right onto the waters bayside and oceanside. Often, nice leafy shaded pedestrian trails run parallel to US1, particularly in areas where the Florida

Keys Overseas Heritage Trail (FKOHT) is completed. The trail helpfully shades walkers from traffic as well as the relentless sun. The FKOHT is planned for the entirety of The Keys, from MM 106 in Key Largo to Key West. Its completion will make a walk of The Florida Keys an even more fantastic experience. At the time of writing, a seventy mile stretch of the FKOHT is completed in segments, with the rest still under construction (https://www.floridastateparks.org/trail/Florida-Keys).

I saw work being undertaken on the FKOHT at various stretches during my walk. The upper part of The Florida Keys is very much complete and I spent large stretches from Key Largo to Islamorada on the shaded Florida Keys Overseas Heritage Trail. Some of the paths in the lower Keys are set within thicker vegetation which on occasion made it preferable for me to walk alongside the road for safety reasons, as a female walking solo.

Walking in The Florida Keys, one will encounter a wealth of wildlife, notably many different species of birds such as great white herons, pelicans, cormorants, frigate birds and ibis - to name just a few. I was amazed at just how close the birds would get to car traffic, obviously being used to motorized traffic noise. Seeing a human, on the other hand, elicited a panic reaction and swift fleeing.

When walking over countless bridges and meeting many fishermen there, it pays to look into their buckets and start a little chat. There is always something to see and something to learn.

Simply taking a moment to look into the water flowing under the many bridges, one can often see a multitude of different species of fish and ocean creatures. I saw many animals this way, including a turtle surfacing in the waters below the 7 Mile Bridge. I also saw dolphins and countless other inhabitants of the ocean going about their daily business. Let's not forget the many land dwellers, some of whom literally crossed my path, such as raccoons, lizards, spiders, snakes and many others.

A little note on the more interesting, and for some perhaps "scarier" inhabitants of the Florida Keys: Florida has some potentially dangerous wildlife and I am not referring to sharks in the water. Most sharks you will see in The Florida Keys are entirely harmless to humans, such as the little bonnet-heads, or nurse sharks feeding on the sandy bottom. However, there are poisonous snakes, alligators and also crocodiles to be aware of. There is no reason to fear these animals. In general, if you don't bother them they won't bother you. However, walkers are well advised to respect the wildlife and not get too close to the animals. Also, feeding of wild animals is generally forbidden for good reason. Crocodiles and alligators that are fed will get too familiar and often aggressive towards humans and subsequently need to be destroyed. Observing the animals from a respectful distance is by far the best course of action. In turn, they will respect us and usually stay well away from humans.

Walking The Keys provides the added benefit of being immersed in nature, yet never too far from civilization. The latter is of course very comforting when attempting a long multi-day walk, even more so when going on a solo walk as a female. I always felt safe knowing that if anything were to happen to me, such as an unlikely snake bite or a (more likely) fall or injury, a quick call would have summoned help within minutes. Having this peace of mind can not be underestimated. Remote areas are so much more dangerous to walk solo.

Due to the topographic nature of The Florida Keys and the roads, namely having to follow the only road (US1), the walk will be alongside noisy traffic on a daily basis, something that is not ideal but can't be helped. In my opinion it is a small price to pay in light of all the sights and rewards along the way. I came to accept the traffic and car drivers as something that would be to my benefit, should I ever have an emergency.

8. The Easy Logistics Of Walking The Florida Keys

In The Keys, one can never really get too far away from civilization. This makes the route along the Overseas Highway much less daunting, especially for first time and solo walkers, who will be comforted by the thought of a store or a doctor only being a phone-call and at most half an hour away. The fast availability of help and provisions proves not only useful in the event of an emergency, but renders the day-to-day management of a long walk so much easier when it comes to supplies and necessities.

I was intensely grateful for the many stores and gas stations along the Overseas Highway, allowing me to only take the bare minimum of food and adequate water supply for the day. This was extremely convenient especially in the first days, as I was not sure exactly how much water I would need to carry. Most importantly, it meant I could keep the weight on my shoulders to a bare minimum. Every little helps, especially during a twenty mile day. Not to forget I was able to treat myself to the occasional luxuries such as a chocolate bar or an ice-cold drink along route - a welcome energy and morale boost on a hot day.

The Florida Keys helped me succeed despite being a sloppily prepared walker, by providing me with plenty of opportunities to obtain more essentials when I ran out of important supplies such as sunscreen, disinfectant, band-aids and other needs. This was one very important factor helping me to complete the walk successfully. It made The Keys by far the most preferable and least stressful route in my vicinity.

Planning this walk of The Florida Keys also made accommodation logistics painless. Not only are The Keys abundant in places to stay, I never had to take a detour away from the Overseas Highway to get to my lodgings. After a long day of walking, it was perfect to be able to overnight along the Overseas

Highway, without having to walk further or backtrack the next morning.

There are, in short, many good reasons why The Florida Keys provide multi-day walkers with a perfect route. They are especially appealing to those who would like to attempt a first walk, or want to walk solo, or don't want to be weighed down by carrying camping equipment.

CHAPTER 3
Planning The Walk

The Florida Keys are perfect for a week long adventure on one's feet. It is of course entirely possible to set off instantly and without much ado: a pair of walking shoes, a backpack, a change of clothes, some provisions and cash will suffice. You won't even need a map, as long as you stay on US1. However, a little planning goes a long way in making the whole experience more enjoyable and less haphazard. Most importantly, good planning ensures the successful completion of a multi-day walk.

How to go about planning and preparing for a long walk?

9. Getting Fit For A Multi-Day Walk

The beauty of walking is this: anyone with two working legs and in general good health can walk. One does not have to be a world class athlete or have any specific training or skill to walk a few miles every day. We might all have a different pace and different fitness level, of course, but that is no reason to put anyone off attempting a multi-day walk.

The terrain in The Florida Keys is easy to manage. There are no mountains or elevations of any kind. The walking surface, on paths or the Overseas Highway, is rarely uneven or challenging and mostly paved. The whole trip can be made in a week by a reasonably fit person. Those wanting to go at a more leisurely pace with some time to relax and soak up some of what The Keys have to offer, can plan on ten to twelve days or more. The speed at which to walk really is up to the individual walker and their fitness level.

There is no denying that one has to have a basic level of fitness and stamina to attempt such a walk, especially when carrying a backpack and even more so when the equipment includes camping gear. In all cases, preparation for a multi-day walk should ideally include some kind of fitness level improvement, as most of us do not routinely walk fifteen to twenty miles per day. At the very least, there needs to be an honest assessment of how many miles one can easily walk per day. Knowing this is imperative when it comes to structuring the days and overnight stays. I would not advise on walking The Florida Keys outside of daylight hours, for example, so a basic fitness assessment and appropriate planning is sensible.

Which exercises help to prepare for a longer walk? It should be obvious: walking, walking and some more walking. As well as walking as much as possible for exercise before a multi-day walk, it is helpful to do some upper body strength exercises to prepare for the added weight of the backpack. This can easily be done by getting into the routine of using the weight machines in the gym twice a week, or by simply adding some push-ups or pull-ups to one's fitness routine. While this is not a necessity, strengthening the upper body and back muscles will certainly help with carrying the backpack.

My personal route to becoming fit for walking The Florida Keys was a little unorthodox, as it entailed doing practically nothing. Having always exercised and been reasonably fit, I was under the (somewhat misguided) impression that it was ok to plan this walk only a couple of weeks before setting off. It turned out I was fine, but certainly could have done with a little more preparation.

In preparation for the walk, I did go on some long walks, around ten to fifteen miles each, on the weekends prior. These walks were not just for 'training' purposes and the walking-in of footwear, but also importantly to determine how many miles I could comfortably walk per day. I then used the approximate figure, which happened to be fifteen to twenty miles in my case, to structure my days and arrange suitable overnight stays without going over my personal maximum mileage of twenty.

I made one crucial mistake: not considering the weight I was going to carry on my shoulders. I had calculated my route and structured my days based on the mileage I could comfortably walk without carrying a backpack. Even without taking any camping gear, the extra weight I was carrying every day amounted to enough to slow me down, as well as causing more wear and tear on my feet and legs than I had expected.

Therefore, I would suggest that you plan on adjusting mileage downwards when carrying a backpack. It is important to bring enough liquids and food. This is of course in addition to a change of shoes, and a few changes of clothing, wet weather gear and whatever else one can not live without. In the end I was lucky: even with the added weight I managed to stick to my schedule, albeit barely. In hindsight, I might have preferred having a less challenging itinerary and adding a day or two to my schedule. Learn from my mistakes and do not overextend yourself. It certainly helps to err on the side of caution and plan in some extra time for inclement weather and emergencies.

To sum up, you do not need to be a fitness freak or athlete to walk The Keys. However, a reasonable level of fitness and some stamina will be required. A long walk over a period of a week or more with a backpack will put quite a strain on anyone's body and joints. Being reasonably fit, I still woke up every day on the walk hurting and having to overcome painful muscles in the first couple of hours of walking. Some discomfort has to be expected. After all, this is going to be a physical challenge and we all know this means: no pain, no gain.

If you need some inspiration, or wonder whether you are fit enough, consider this: in 1955, a lady by the name of Mrs. Gatewood became the first woman to hike the entire 2168 mile Appalachian trail, wearing tennis shoes and foraging for food along the way. She left with a little sack of supplies and no tent or sleeping bag. Mrs. Gatewood was 67 years old at the time of the walk and went on to do even more long-distance hiking well into her 70's, sometimes averaging twenty two miles per day.

Just reflect on this for one moment. When I read about her, I immediately felt disappointed in my achievement. What the heck was I doing, writing about a 105 mile walk, a mere joke compared to what this lady accomplished at such an advanced age (*Grandma Gatewood's Walk: The Inspiring Story Of The Woman Who Saved The Appalachian Trail* (2014) by Ben Montgomery).

Now, after some time to ponder this, I see it a little differently. Her story should serve us all as great inspiration. However small or big the challenge of a walk we set ourselves, in the end the distance makes little difference. I know she must have gotten up every morning, tired and with aching limbs, probably asking herself "what am I doing here?" Every day she started anew and set her mind to just get on with it. This is what it takes: having the mindset to carry on, one foot in front of the other, never giving up – whether it is a ten mile walk, a 105 mile walk, or indeed a 2168 mile walk of the Appalachian Trail. Walks are made up of single steps. Let Mrs. Gatewood's story be your inspiration, whatever your age or your limitations. You can do it too!

10. Clothing And Equipment

I already touched a little on equipment and clothing in the preceding chapters. After an accurate assessment of one's fitness level and some training, having the right equipment is probably the second biggest factor in ensuring a successful completion of a multi-day walk. The equipment doesn't need to be fancy but it should be functional, practical and as lightweight as possible. I made a number of mistakes, which I hope you can avoid.

Mistake 1: I wore cotton T-shirts.

It doesn't sound like a crime, but in this case it turned out to be a mistake that I very much regretted. Being an avid cotton lover, there was no convincing me that man-made fiber could in any way, shape or form be superior to my beloved cotton. After the first hour of walking The Keys, I had to admit much to my chagrin: I had been wrong. Worse, I had to live with the discomfort for the rest of the walk.

My advice regarding clothing applies to walking just about anywhere in warm weather for a longer distance. If like me, you insist on wearing your beloved cotton, this will happen: perspiration will eventually - in The Florida Keys within approximately five minutes - soak your shirts and you will spend the rest of the day in wet clothes. This proves extremely uncomfortable as well as unhealthy. It pays off to invest in some moisture wicking active-wear T-shirts and shorts, at least for the walking part of the day. Console yourself with the thought that you may change into cotton shirts in the evening when relaxing.

Mistake 2: I underestimated the sun.

Walking in the tropics, I was very cognizant of needing (and applying frequently) a good high factor sunscreen. This is definitely a must-have on your list, unless you want to burn to a crisp and be in pain from day 1 onwards, as well as return home looking like a prune. All joking apart, your best friend will be a tube of good sunscreen and these two words: apply frequently. Even if you decide to walk in a more northerly location in the summertime, always take and apply sunscreen. Our modern day mollycoddled skin is simply not used to being exposed to sunlight for six to eight hours daily, unless perhaps you work outside for a living and are already a prune.

I had not anticipated that despite repeated application of sunscreen factor 30, my skin would sport a leathery tan from the third day onwards. Being exposed to tropical sun for eight hours a day is too much, even with a good sunscreen. My main mistake here was not bringing and wearing long sleeved shirts. Eventually, you will need and want to cover up. Bring long-sleeved lightweight shirts. Other must-have items are good sunglasses and a hat. I did not take a hat, which was bad judgment on my behalf, but at least I had a visor to cut out the glare and keep my face shaded, which helped immensely. The Keys route has long stretches without shade and the sun on your head all day will feel brutal.

Mistake 3: I believed bug-spray would save me.

Forget it. You might as well save yourself and your skin from all the chemicals and just give up and let them feast on you. They will anyway, especially if you are a mosquito magnet like me. You are likely a magnet if you suffer with bites even when nobody else in the vicinity does. By "suffer", I refer to the ratio of bites found on mosquito magnets as opposed to other people being roughly 20:1 in my experience. This figure is approximate and results from years of involuntary studies and research undertaken by the long-suffering author. In fact, this research started in childhood when on vacations and sleeping in one room with my family. I often woke up in the mornings wondering why I looked like having contracted the bubonic plague, while the rest of my family did not sport a single bite.

There are also the psychological scars of being a mosquito magnet: one main characteristic is the desire to strangle anyone who pipes up: "oh I just don't feel them anymore". If this sentence turns you red with rage, you are sure to be one of us, the twenty percent of mosquito magnets. You and I both know it's not that the lucky ones "don't feel them". The plain truth is that they just don't get bitten.

In any case, mosquito magnet or not, one thing is for sure: the bugs will find you. You may of course spray Deet all over your body to test my theory, and find the mosquitos and famous no-see-ums (I'll get to those later) coughing a little maybe, yet undeterred from their main purpose: to make your life and your skin an itchy and bumpy hell.

I practically bathed in Deet to see if it would help. Guess what? My little buzzing friends bit my fingers, ears, toes and through my clothing, as if to remind me of all the places that were lacking Deet coverage. After a while I felt they were mocking me. Don't even get me started on the no-see-ums - so called because they are tiny and stealth, so you don't "see-um". They hunted me down ad nauseam, with their little bites lingering like an itchy souvenir for two weeks after the walk. I counted about ninety bites when I arrived in Key West.

I am sure many other parts of the world have their unpleasant critters making your life uncomfortable. It comes with spending a lot of time in nature. Especially when camping, it is tough to get away from them, so do what you can to cover up/spray or whatever you think is appropriate. Unfortunately, as I had a pretty tight schedule, my walks often began in twilight (the mosquito hour), and there was just no getting away from them. I had to "suck it up" while they sucked my blood.

Mistake 4: I believed with adequate preparation I would be blister and pain free.

I had made sure that all my footwear was very well walked-in. I am not silly. I took shoes and sandals that had already been in my possession for some time and made sure to wear them whilst training for the walk. I was therefore convinced my feet would be just fine. I had not taken into account, however, how much more wear and tear the weight of the backpack would add. Additionally, I had never walked a full six to eight hours a day in training. The morale of the story is: do not take brand new walking boots or trekking sandals but make sure you have worn them in well. Expect previously unimaginable levels of wear and tear on your feet. Just be prepared for this and accept it. I found wearing two pairs of socks helpful for preventing blisters, although in the end blisters are inevitable. Therefore, take plenty of band aids, possibly even bandages and definitely disinfectant, to make sure you can tend to your feet adequately at the end of each day. They will thank you and help to achieve your goal of finishing the walk successfully.

I could not finish this chapter about equipment and clothing without adding a paragraph or two about the backpack. Your backpack is going to be your best friend for the entire trip, holding all your necessities. I suggest on using a good backpack rather than a push cart (which I briefly discuss below), especially when not camping. It is by far the easiest and most effortless way to carry belongings when on trails or walking on a narrow path by the side of the road. It pays off getting a backpack that fits your height and is adjustable. The backpack should also have a sturdy reinforced back for an ergonomic weight distribution. It doesn't need to be expensive, as long as it fits comfortably and is fit for the purpose.

I decided to use the smallest backpack I could get away with, to fit in all the essentials and nothing more. This is a mind trick I use on myself, suffering from chronic "overpackitis". Having backpacked before, I am driven by the inexplicable desire to fill a backpack to the brim, no matter how big it is. I did not want to get tempted to carry anything unnecessary. It worked out well for me to get the smallest backpack appropriate for this length of trip, with a volume of around forty liters.

In certain instances, you might consider using a push cart instead of a backpack. Walking The Keys is by no means a serious long-distance endurance hike, as it can be done in a week. However, if you are planning on something much longer or have back problems, you might want to use a push cart or stroller instead of a backpack. I have heard of some cross country hikers who have successfully used a push cart and found this much easier and even a necessity for carrying enough water through remote desert regions. In fact, a push cart or better, a stroller, would work in The Florida Keys as well, provided it is narrow enough to maneuver narrow paths and the side of the road. This might be interesting to note for persons with back problems who have shied away from a multi-day walk because they are unable to carry a heavy backpack all day.

To conclude my suggestions regarding equipment, here is my personal list of essentials to take on a week-long walk of The Florida Keys:

- Lightweight breathable T-shirts, long sleeved shirts, pants, shorts and lots of changes of underwear and socks.
- Food (energy bars, nuts, etc.) and plenty of water for the day.
- A hat with wide rim.
- A good pair of sunglasses, consider polarized lenses.
- Toiletries (a good deodorant will be your best friend).

- Two pairs of walking shoes and a pair of light flip flops for relaxing in the evenings.
- A foldable waterproof poncho and waterproof cover for the backpack.
- An umbrella for staying dry and for shade.
- Sunscreen – high factor.
- After-Sun lotion or body lotion.
- Insect repellant.
- Basic first aid kit with plenty of band-aids, disinfectant, bandages, something for bug bites, antihistamine and painkillers, your medications.
- Phone and, if needed, a camera and iPad/Kindle (don't forget the chargers).
- Maps or GPS (not a necessity but helpful).
- Camping equipment, if camping.
- Cash, especially 1 dollar bills and coins for vending machines, tips etc.
- The one thing you can't live without, unless it weighs more than a pair of shoes.

11. Where To Stay In The Florida Keys – Hotel Versus Camping

I have come across walkers who insisted on camping during multi-day walks. On the flip side I have also encountered many people who preferred staying in hotels. There is no right or wrong way to spend your nights and it will come down to personal preference.

Hotels/Motels along the Overseas Highway

Making use of motels along the Overseas Highway was my personal preferred option for three main reasons:

1. Safety: As a female walking solo, I was careful to cut risks to my safety down to the bare minimum. I did not feel comfortable camping alone, so I didn't even consider it.

2. Comfort: I assumed that after a day of fifteen miles or more of walking under the hot Florida sun, I would appreciate a nice shower and a soft bed. In hindsight, this was a very good decision. A nice clean and soft bed was something I began to look forward to every single day, almost like a reward. I would certainly have been much less enthusiastic to see this walk through if I had needed to put up a tent and roll out the sleeping bag after walking all day. I don't know about you, but I am a girl after all, and I needed some basic comforts after a day's slogging.

3. Less Equipment To Carry: The third reason is pretty obvious. Camping gear adds a lot of weight, no matter how lightweight a tent and sleeping bag might be. In the end, I was angry with every ounce of water unconsumed at the end of the day, as I would have carried it all day in vain. Carrying camping gear certainly would have added a few days to my walk. All that extra weight will slow you down considerably.

There are plenty of hotels and motels along the Overseas Highway. I decided not to make suggestions here as everybody has a different opinion of what constitutes a good place to stay, based on individual expectations and cost. I was on a tight budget and stayed in a couple of places that most likely won't be graced with my presence again. At the end of each day, I was always happy and grateful for a shower and a clean bed, no matter how simple the accommodation.

Planning overnight stays comes down to how many miles you are prepared to walk each day. Your individual walking "radius" will limit the places suitable for an overnight stay. You will likely walk longer stretches on some days and much shorter stretches on other days, depending on where you can find suitable overnight accommodation and camping sites.

In The Florida Keys, it can be somewhat complicated to find a place to overnight close to the 7 Mile Bridge. On the bridge and beyond, the walking route is uninhabited for a considerable number of miles. The next possible overnight lodging when coming from Marathon is the Big Pine Key Fishing Lodge. This makes for a hefty 17 mile stretch walk from the beginning of the 7 Mile Bridge in Marathon. Unsurprisingly, this stretch was one of my longest walking days (20 miles), as my accommodation was located in the center of Big Pine Key. When stretching one's walking limits, like I did in this instance, it makes sense to schedule the following day a little easier with a much lower mileage, if possible.

If you are planning on staying in hotels and motels along the way, do not get tempted to "wing" it. It is absolutely advisable to book ahead. This will not only keep your wallet happier (the best prices are usually available well in advance), but also save you from running out of options of places to stay. The Florida Keys are a very well known and popular vacation destination for visitors from all over the world, especially during winter months. Depending on the season, it can be almost impossible to get a room even as far as a month in advance. This is particularly true for Key West in winter season or with any kind of special event in the islands, such as the famous Fantasy Fest in October. Plan well in advance if you can, and especially if you are tempted to come for Fantasy Fest. You are wondering what Fantasy Fest is? In essence, Fantasy Fest is: plenty of people (many past their prime) completely butt naked except for a smidgen of body paint, having a great time.

Camping

I am certainly not going to stop anyone from lugging their own camping equipment across the Overseas Highway, or across whichever other route they have chosen. You won't find me doing it. I am not a fan of camping. However, it is true that in many places outside of The Florida Keys, if you are planning on a multi-day walk, camping may be a necessity. In more remote areas, there simply won't be any alternative accommodation on some stretches.

As we have already established, the added weight of camping equipment needs to be considered. Unless you are a seriously fit and strong person – and even then – walking twenty miles per day with camping equipment is going to take most of the enjoyment out of a walk, unless you see it as some sort of boot camp exercise. If you are embarking on a long walk for contemplation and inspiration, forget it. Your mind will mostly be focused on trying to make the schedule and coping with the aches and pains you will get from pushing your body too hard.

The question is: how much should you lower your daily mileage count when carrying camping equipment? The answer of course depends on personal preference and fitness, but I know anything over fifteen miles per day was hard going for me even without carrying any extra equipment. Therefore, I would aim to stay below fifteen miles with the added weight of camping gear. This is just a suggestion, of course, but trust me: it's a good one!

There are plenty of camp sites in The Florida Keys and whilst walking, I came across many of them, some looking positively enticing. For the same reasons as I do not want to recommend hotels, I hesitate to recommend individual camp sites. I did not try any, after all. However, I would like to draw attention to these stunning State Parks with camp sites: John Pennekamp Coral Reef State Park, Long Key State Park, Bahia Honda State Park, as well as Sugarloaf KOA (there are also cabins for rent here) and Boyd's Key West Campground. I would probably include some or all of these in my planning if I were to camp, which I am not and I won't, but don't let me stop you.

A quick glance at the map reveals that the camp sites and State Parks are way too unevenly spaced to make for easy planning. However, there are some RV sites where you may be able to camp. In the planning stages, it might be useful to approach the owners or management and explain, as oftentimes an exception can be made even if there isn't any "official" camping. The beauty of The Keys community is that most people are more than willing to help. Perhaps also consider Airbnb for something unusual, and particularly if one of the objectives of the walk is to meet local people. In The Florida Keys it is possible to stay on a boat with Airbnb. How fun. I don't know how practical it would be to go down that route, but it would surely be an unforgettable experience to stay for a night or two on a sailboat for the whole "Keys Experience".

If you are tempted to try the cheapest option of all and camp by the side of the road, I strongly discourage this. As well as not having any facilities at your disposal, which would be depressing after a day's toiling and perspiring across miles of dusty road, you could get yourself arrested. I guess this has the potential of making your walk of The Florida Keys a little more "interesting", but is it really worth it? I suggest not. As far as I am concerned, it always pays off to stay within the bounds of legality and respect your surroundings and the community.

To conclude the hotels versus camping conundrum: Whether to stay at a hotel or camp site or a combination of the two is essentially up to personal preference. It is all perfectly possible and enjoyable when attempting to walk The Florida Keys. Whatever the preference, be sure to research your route and plan it out in detail – most importantly the amount of miles you can comfortably walk in a day – and then plan your accommodation or camping sites accordingly and well in advance.

12. How To Structure Walking Days

It is certainly advisable to structure the days and plan the walking time for each day on a multi-day long distance walk. This will help to stay on schedule as well as ensuring enough rest and recovery time every day, in order to feel adequately energized for the next.

My plan was to walk between fifteen to twenty miles on average a day, which amounted to six to eight hours of walking. When walking in a warmer climate, it pays off to walk more than half of the daily mileage in the morning. As the day wears on, the ground soaks up the rays of the sun. By the afternoon this heat will be reflected from the ground thus adding degrees to the "felt" temperatures, especially when walking on or near asphalt. This, together with fatigue setting in, makes walking in the afternoon hours all the more exhausting. Also, storms are more likely in the afternoon hours and you might have to sit them out, especially if there is lightning, so it does pay off to start early.

As a result of the heat, I certainly needed more time per mile in the afternoons. I usually started walking at or before 8am, after a light breakfast. I then attempted to put the first few hours and miles behind me at a good pace. The aim was to have more than half of my daily mileage walked before 1pm, so I would be able to have a good rest for lunch.

The average person's walking speed is roughly three miles per hour. I found out during the walk, that it was more realistic to calculate my walking speed at around 2.5 miles per hour with a backpack. How to structure the day is a personal decision, but I was extremely happy to arrive at my lodgings between 3pm and 5pm. This meant arriving in daylight hours and being able to have a good rest each evening.

Arriving at my lodgings by late afternoon also gave me plenty of time to relax, reflect and explore my surroundings a little, if I wanted to. Don't forget to add a mile or two to your tally at the end of the day. You will need to walk again if you want to eat, and especially if you are looking for the comfort of a cooked meal and a little socializing to reward yourself. I certainly enjoyed that aspect of the walk, having some time to unwind at the end of the day, together with a good meal and some journaling. Often, getting out and about again, despite aching limbs, resulted in meeting and chatting to some interesting local people. If you want to walk The Keys to happiness, be sure to include enough down-time to enjoy and appreciate everything and everyone around you.

Interestingly, I noticed the last mile or two of the walking day always stretching into infinity, whether it was a fifteen or twenty mile day. It seemed to happen once I realized the day was "conquered" with only a couple of miles left to walk. Those couple of miles then might take me an hour or two. I definitely noticed slowing down as the day went on. Towards the end of the day, feet start to hurt and the upper body will feel tired from a day of carrying the backpack. It seems the mind meanwhile is already focused on the shower, food and a nice bed ahead. I guess it's psychological.

Here is how I structured my days:

- Wake up early, have a quick breakfast and out on the road by 8am at the latest, starting off the walk at a good pace.
- Lunch around 12noon or 1pm, after ten miles or more of walking. Twenty to thirty minute break and a light lunch.
- Arrival at the overnight accommodation between 3pm and 5:30pm for a little relaxation and a shower.
- Finding somewhere to eat between 6-7pm unless I was too tired or there was nothing close-by (it helps to carry some provisions for those days).
- In bed by 10:30 for a good night's rest.

Structuring my days like this certainly worked for me. I never once had to walk in the dark or was unable to keep to my schedule.

13. A Note On Safety For Female Solo Walkers

This topic is close to my heart. I particularly like doing things alone, especially walking and traveling. In fact, I find it meditative and stimulating. Admittedly, it is hard to marry the wish to walk longer distances alone with the need for personal safety, especially as a woman.

Having embarked on plenty of smaller walks over a day or weekend by myself, the topic of safety has always been at the forefront of my mind. Some walks have led me through urban and suburban areas, others through relative wilderness. Different localities come with different challenges to personal safety. In urban and suburban areas we mostly deal with people, most of whom are pleasant or neutral, while there could be the odd one who may wish us harm. In more remote areas we may have to deal with the forces of nature or wildlife, which can become a threat. Everyone who has ever been without a shelter in a deep wood or open area during a bad thunderstorm can attest to this. We don't have much influence on natural events other than being prepared with adequate gear. Hence here I focus on the personal safety aspect, especially for solo walkers and from the female perspective.

The Florida Keys are a fairly safe route to walk for many reasons. There are no long stretches without settlements and stores, and most of the terrain is open, which makes for great visibility. I felt reasonably safe by walking on the side of the main road and I would recommend this to any other female solo walkers. Stay visible and don't walk along paths that are overgrown and can not be seen from the main road. It is tempting to get away from traffic. The lovely Florida Keys Overseas Heritage Trail provides the walker with a shaded path right next to the road, especially in the higher Keys, which is the ideal solution. In the lower Keys, those parts of the Overseas Heritage Trail that are finished, often run through higher and thicker vegetation and further away from the road.

In those instances, in the interest of personal safety, I decided to skip the trail and walk right along the side of the main road and towards oncoming traffic (as is the rule). It was not always the most pleasant way to walk but I did consider it as the safest option, being a solo female walker.

One could argue that it is also dangerous to walk close to car traffic. This is true. However, the risk can be minimized, which leads me to the next safety tip for anyone and especially females: please plan your days out in a way that you never have to walk outside of daylight hours. I learnt on the first day how dangerous this is, whether by the side of the road or on a path. Walking in the dark is not only a threat to your personal safety, it also bears the risk of injury from uneven paths and obstructions or holes, and of course there is the traffic. It borders on a death wish walking alongside the main road in the dark. If you do run the risk of getting caught out by darkness, you must at least carry a reflective vest and a flashlight.

I did get warned by several people that The Florida Keys have certain "characters" I would wish to avoid as a female walking by myself. I am pretty sure every place has those characters. This does not mean we should worry about it incessantly, but it certainly makes a strong case for only walking in daylight and close to the road where one is visible. These two simple tips should cut out most potential dangers to any female wanting to walk The Florida Keys solo.

I stayed in motels along the Overseas Highway not just for comfort but also for safety. While some may be comfortable camping alone as a female in The Keys, I would not have been. Again, it is up to the individual, but if you want to cut threats to your personal safety down to a minimum, I would advise to stay in motels or at least camp at busy camp sites and near well-lit areas.

There are various products marketed as self defense solutions for women, such as pepper spray and stunning devices. Carrying such a device is a good idea, if only to feel safer for having it. I did not carry one and even if I had, I would not have had a reason to use one on this walk. I was lucky. When embarking on the walk, it crossed my mind several times that it would have been sensible to have at least pepper spray with me. Lacking any alternatives, I might have tried to use bug spray (directed at the face/eyes) to keep someone at bay. Presumably this would have been better than nothing. It should go without saying that when walking solo, a phone is an absolute necessity for anyone.

The best defense of all: your intuition. There were a couple of times when my intuition told me to hurry on past a person or to get away from an overgrown path back onto the main road. I listened to my intuition and was fine, without any incidents. I never felt scared or threatened during my walk.

To sum it up, here are the points I consider good practice when walking solo:

- Always stay aware of your surroundings, keep eyes and ears open and be alert.
- Walk only within daylight hours.
- Carry a phone and keep it charged.
- Walk alongside the main road or in open areas where you are visible and you have good visibility.
- Take a deterrent such as pepper spray or a stunning device.
- Stay in hotels/motels or when camping alone, put your tent up in a busy/well lit area with other people close by.
- Trust your intuition.

Life is risk. The mere fact that you are getting "out there" as a solo female (or male) undoubtedly involves a certain amount of risk.

It is possible to minimize the risk with sensible planning and by taking precautions. However, we also have to trust that all will be well and take on a walk with positive thoughts rather than fear-based thoughts. Being overly suspicious and scared can rob us of wonderful experiences with well-meaning strangers along the way. My advice would be to be sensible by all means, but there is no reason to be fearful or overly suspicious. A walk is supposed to be fun, after all.

CHAPTER 4

Planning And Walking The Keys: Day By Day Account

I started the walk in late October 2013, with a ride to Key Largo on the Greyhound bus and 105 miles ahead of me. I had no idea of all the adventures and sights I would come across. Least of all did I expect to end the walk with a celebration in the southernmost strip-club of the USA.

14. Planning The Keys Walk

It was "just an idea" at first. I love to walk and I love The Keys - in my mind this had to be a winning combination. I had never walked more than seventeen miles on one day hikes and without a backpack. Would I let that lack of experience stop me? Perhaps it should have, or at least inspired me to do some serious preparation and training first. However, being a naturally impatient and impulsive person, it didn't stop me from planning a walk as soon as possible. Once I had made up my mind, the planning began in earnest.

Firstly, I wanted to collect some information. I felt curious as to whether people had walked The Florida Keys before, how long it took them and any other information I could lay my hands on. I proceeded to contact The Keys Tourist Agency for information and perhaps some encouragement. I needed it. After all, I might be the first woman ever to walk The Keys alone. A few exchanges via email later, I understood that there wasn't much interest in walkers though I did receive a courteous reply when asking for information and help. To me, it seemed like a missed PR opportunity to showcase the Florida Keys Overseas Heritage Trail for walkers.

Next on the planning list: arranging affordable accommodation. I began to write to a few hotels and motels, asking whether they wanted to support "possibly the first female to walk The Keys unaided". Coming up with a great pitch was clearly not one of my strong-points. I decided to use the word "possibly", in case one or more ladies would appear from the woodwork claiming that they had done it already. I had done some research and had not found any information about a woman walking The Florida Keys solo, but was well aware that this doesn't mean it never happened.

Perhaps not entirely surprising: I got no replies, with the exception of one from Edgewater Lodge. I had started to feel a little deflated. No real encouraging response from Keys Tourism followed by no responses from lodgings, when suddenly I received a very encouraging email from Edgewater Lodge pledging their support. This not only made me very happy, it also strengthened my resolve to go for it. Edgewater Lodge was situated slap bang in the middle of The Florida Keys.

After some emails back and forth, it transpired that Edgewater Lodge was not only going to help by giving me a discounted room rate, no. They went above and beyond all expectations and pledged to provide a room for one night completely free of charge. A strange feeling of trepidation as well as huge sense of gratitude came over me. How the heck could I possibly cancel the walk now, having been offered a free room? My conscience wouldn't allow that. I couldn't let them down or look like a fool, could I? My mind was pretty much made up. For better or worse: I was going! It was the encouragement I needed to firm up my plans from probable to definite.

Uplifted by the generous offering of Edgewater Lodge, I found some other reasonable accommodations along the route and my schedule began to take shape. I planned on walking between fifteen to twenty miles per day from motel to motel. I had never done anything like this before, so I scoured the internet and found various accounts of men who had walked The Florida Keys. One of the accounts gave me some good information, but it also served to fuel some doubts, as I read about poisonous snakes and the "scary" 7 Mile Bridge.

Having to carry a backpack suddenly started to worry me. Especially when I found out that one the gentlemen I was referring to, carried no equipment except for a camera and water. The lucky man had a wife with a support car. Walking the Florida Keys had taken him one day longer than I was planning on, and suddenly I was filled with dread. I did not have a wife (or husband for that matter) with support car ready at the finishing line at the end of each day.

There would be nobody to wipe the pearls of sweat from my face, hand me a cold drink and say "there, there". What if I couldn't make it? I would let the nice people at Edgewater Lodge down, as well as all my friends who were now aware of my plans and had started to cheer me on. Worse, it would catapult me right back to my hopeless, depressed and uninspired mental state. Imagine, I would be the woman that "attempted" to walk The Keys but never actually finished. Oh dear. I felt a little stupid and discouraged. I had set myself a pretty tight schedule. Well, it was done, the accommodation booked and my backpack was packed. For better or worse, I was ready to set off on 27th October 2013.

On a side note, you might have noticed by now that I haven't said a peep about the route I was about to embark on. Why not? There is only one. Most of you will know there is but one main road in and out of Key West, the Overseas Highway (or US1), ending at the famous Mile 0 in Key West. At least I had one thing going for me: there was no chance of getting lost.

15. Arrival At Key Largo

As I found myself on the Greyhound bus down to Key Largo, I had ample time to reflect on the past few weeks. I had not been happy over losing my job and having to start again, plus my dating life didn't look inspiring either. I felt very down. To top it off, I had just dumped my MoM (Man of the Moment) at the Greyhound bus station. A couple of weeks prior to me setting off, he had suggested for us to spend a romantic weekend in Key West, to celebrate the end of the walk. Instead, so he informed me in the car on the way to the station, the plans were off. Apparently, MoM had to feed his ex-girlfriend's cats. My ears were ringing. I felt the heat rising from my stomach into my throat and finally into my head. He talked some more but all I saw was his mouth opening and closing, occasionally I could make out sentences like "cats with special diets" and "they are like children to her" or "she only trusts me". I exploded into a verbal barrage fueled by disbelief and anger.

This surely had to rank pretty high on the list of "most blood-boiling things any woman could possibly hear from a boyfriend" anytime, but especially so when that woman is just about to set off on a somewhat scary challenge all by herself. After exploding, I dumped him there and then and theatrically stomped off into the general direction of the Greyhound bus. I couldn't believe my ears. What a cheek. Here he was, telling me he was going to look after another woman's pussy, and trying to justify it rationally. It was infuriating and I was infuriated.

I suddenly remembered a T-shirt I once saw with the print: "who has the pussy has the power". I never thought in my wildest dreams that this image would one day haunt me. I remember giving him a choice before storming off: the pussies or me! Much to my horror and disbelief, the decision was not made in my favor. So I made mine. MoM was henceforth MoP (Man of the Past). May he choke on a hairball.

Sitting on the bus, I was feeling angry and sad rather than excited. I was dwelling on all the negative things that had happened. Apart from anything else, now I did not even have the prospect of a fun weekend with my (now ex-) date in Key West. Getting closer to Key Largo, tears were running down my cheeks. Oh no, this wasn't how I had pictured the beginning of the walk. Why was I feeling so bad? Was it the dark thoughts of the last few weeks, the dumping, or the nerves and the doubts? I should be excited. Then, as we crossed the first bridge into Key Largo and I saw the turquoise blue waters, boats and birds circling, everything changed. It was so pretty, I could no longer help but feel excited and cheerful.

I arrived at the Key Largo Greyhound bus stop, which is situated roughly half-way down Key Largo at around Mile Marker 99. They are not very flexible about their stops, so my only choice was to hop out there and back-track to Mile Marker 105. I was determined to walk The Florida Keys, and wanted to walk all, which for me entailed walking most of Key Largo and not just half. Back up I went…

As I arrived at my lodgings, I felt exhausted and incredibly keen to get to my room. The emotional episode in Fort Lauderdale plus my first walk in the afternoon heat with my backpack, even if amounting to only six miles, had already taken its toll. My feet complained and my excitement gave way to the suspicion that I was in fact entirely crazy and unprepared to embark on this walk. It occurred to me that I had at least a couple of twenty mile days planned "down the road". Here was me massaging my sore feet after six miles. This did not bode well.

I could think of nothing but a lie-down in my room. Looking forward to a quick check-in at the motel, I envisaged it like this: sign name, take the key and go. I couldn't have been more wrong. I had entered The Florida Keys and was soon made aware of the fact that people and clocks here tick on island time. I had entered a different time zone and not only did the clocks tick more slowly, but once the locals detected you were in a rush, the clocks came to a grinding halt. Getting to my room as quickly as possible? What was I thinking?

The first thing the owner of the little motel said, after "hello" and mustering me from head to toe, was: "sit down". I did as I was told. Awkwardly, with my backpack still on, I sat down teetering on the edge of the seat, determined that this would not be my stopping place for long. He then asked me a set of questions, along the lines of "Walking The Keys? Alone?", after which he determined that I was a little crazy. I had come to that conclusion myself already, I told him, but it wasn't going to deter me from trying. He seemed satisfied by that answer and proceeded with some well-meaning and rather sweet advice.

It now dawned on me that much more time would likely pass before I might retire to the room. He meant well and started off with some general life and job advice ending with: "we have a German lady staying with us, I will introduce you, maybe she has some advice". Then came a little talk about The Florida Keys, which mostly consisted of him telling me how much trash I would see by the side of the road. Apparently, he interviewed a pair of walkers who had stayed at his motel, about their main impression from the walk. Their answer: a lot of trash by the side of the road. Wonderful, I thought, was this supposed to be uplifting on the eve of my week long challenge? Maybe he was trying to lower my expectations, or save me from my crazy walk?

The owner of the little motel was not finished. I was ceremonially handed a pile of coupon books. Incidentally, those were weighing me down the next day, as I had not dared throw them in the trash for fear he would find them there and be upset or chase me down, thinking I had forgotten them. Yes, I am a people pleaser.

Finally, I decided to make a go of it at a little pause in conversation, grabbed the key and got up, when the owner quickly said: "we are not finished yet, sit back down". With a big thump, the sound of defeat, my backpack and I slumped back into the chair. I did as I was told - again.

He happily informed me that I was lucky to get an upgrade to a better room. However, there would be a little problem with the room, he said. The motel owner then explained that the TV was not working, asking: "would that be a problem?" I opened my mouth wanting to tell him that I didn't need an upgraded room. Before I could get a word in, he went on to say that if it was a problem, sadly, there wouldn't be much he could do about it. He informed me that he was not a TV fixer man, therefore the TV would remain broken for the duration of my stay. I closed my mouth again, briefly wondering why he would "upgrade" me to a room with faulty equipment, but by then my life had virtually been sucked out of me. I could not have cared less about a TV. In fact, he could have told me I would be sleeping in a cave or a tree house, I just wanted those keys and my room for once and all. He had talked me into submission, defeat, capitulation even. I thanked him for the upgrade and assured him I would not be calling and complaining about the TV.

He finally seemed satisfied and I was allowed to get up and move. The motel owner then gave me a complete narrated tour of the room, finishing with: "and to your left the TV, which is not working". Just as I was beginning to think this was a Monty Python sketch, or candid camera, I was dragged outside again to be introduced to the German lady. She was already in her pajamas (at 5pm) and looked somewhat bedraggled, as well as perturbed at this – clearly unwanted – intrusion of her home from home.

A courteous "oh hello" was exchanged as well as a handshake, after which she hurried back inside, never to be seen again. Perfect networking for introverts, I thought. Well, it had been sweet of him to make such an effort to connect me with my countrywoman.

Finally I was in my dark and dated room with leaking plumbing and yes, of course, the broken TV. I briefly wondered what the other room would have looked like, a downgrade seemed hard to imagine. I didn't really care. There was a clean and comfortable bed.

No sooner had I put my head on the pillow, my stomach started to rumble ominously. How inconvenient. Off I went again, up and down the Overseas Highway, the road that was to be my permanent travel companion for the next week, in search of something edible. Oh calamity, everything close-by was shut. Quite a way down on the Overseas Highway, at least another mile south, I found a small Mexican roadside café and got mildly excited when I saw it was open. This would do nicely! I peeked inside and found a scene that looked like a saloon from a 1970s Spaghetti Western:

It was dark with ceiling fans busily circulating air as thick as pea soup. The air-conditioning was bust, and must have been for some time. The "regulars" at the bar and tables either knew each other too well to make conversation, or were paralyzed from the lack of air-conditioning: not a word was spoken, heads hung low over plates. The door creaked as I slowly opened it a little wider and all eyes turned on me. More silence. Only the humming of the fans and the cook/waitress, chopping up something non-descript, interrupted the painful silence:

Hum... chop, chop, chop... hum.

I so wanted a younger (actually much younger) version of Clint Eastwood jump out of a corner to scoop me up and away, preferably to an air-conditioned Steakhouse. Alas, no such luck. I crept backwards out of the place, trying to close the door quietly. Oh well, I had wanted to sit outside anyway. In fact, I wondered why people were inside at all, with broken air-conditioning and pea soup air. I marveled at the nice and almost crisp late October air I found outside. Ah, how lovely!

It quickly became apparent just why I was the only person sitting outside. Within minutes, a little cloud of blood-suckers circled me, trying to find a suitable landing spot. It was mosquito o'clock in Key Largo and I was for dinner.

I did what had to be done and what undoubtedly many generations of Keys residents had done before me: ordered a drink and accepted the presence of little swamp angels with grace. Well, with as much grace as I could muster in between swatting and cursing. Seemingly, having a drink in peace wasn't going to be easy, as now the waitress distracted me from my killing spree, demanding my ID. I mumbled something about being nearly forty – no reaction from her – and grumpily pulled my ID out of the bag with one hand whilst swatting mosquitos with the other, eliciting a heavily accented comment of pity from her: "ah, mosquitos, so sorry, is bad outside."

As I sat there with blood stains screaming murder all over my legs, pondering on what tomorrow would look like with already blistered feet and swelling mosquito bites, a big dog saunters past my table. He was unattended with the leash dragging on the ground. The dog was swiftly followed by a handsome stranger, who introduced himself as Steve, and asked whether he could join me at my table. Things were looking up, I thought. Little did I know that the thought of "things looking up" would become quite the Freudian slip.

Steve was not the shy sort, as I soon found out. Without much introduction, or small talk, he immediately started to share his experiences with no less than: female ejaculation. I listened silently, trying not to look shocked, whilst swatting more mosquitos. On account of the conversation topic the swatting had become a nervous reaction. I was wondering: why always me? I had hoped for some civilized conversation. Was that too much to ask for?

I ordered another drink. Alcohol was a solution after all. While he cheerfully continued his talk about other people's bodily fluids, I topped up my fluids whilst plotting an escape. I was still intent on keeping an open mind, but then Steve uttered the word "squirt". Enough was enough. I was done with the topic of female ejaculation once and for all and assertively took the conversation into my own hands. My conversation topic now revolved around engineering a swift escape. I excused myself on account of having an early start the next morning.

I assumed Steve was harmless, even though he did fish for being invited into my hotel room. He knew I was going to disappoint him but probably felt obliged to try just in case I wanted to find out about the practical aspects of his favorite and clearly much studied topic. I certainly did not!

Being a gentleman, Steve would not let me walk back alone in the dark. His motorcycle had a dog-cage, plus I was not intent on riding with a stranger who was interested in rather strange topics of conversation. We agreed on me having Jack, his dog, for an escort back to my lodgings.

Steve got onto his motorcycle to meet me down the road. The dog, clearly worried that his master had abandoned him, got faster and faster and pulled me like a child behind him. When I arrived at my motel, frazzled, he was already there to claim Jack and we said our good byes. When we had met at the little eatery earlier, Steve had been on the way to Key West for Fantasy Fest but ended up sacrificing those plans for our little dinner rendezvous. He was still headed down south, however, and cheerfully declared: "We might meet again on the Overseas Highway." We did not, but the thought of meeting my handsome stranger and his little friend again made me smile.

16. Day 1: Key Largo Mile Marker 103 To Islamorada Via Tavernier (18 Miles)

This was my first full day of walking, a whole eighteen miles to my next stop in Islamorada. I set off with no coffee and no breakfast, munching on a little cereal bar whilst walking. I inspected the package. It showed a man climbing up a cliff, which seemed appropriate. Key Largo, although as flat as can be, did indeed seem like a cliff to climb. It is not only the northernmost Key but also the largest.

I did not dare to stop anywhere for fear of losing time. This being my first day, I had no idea at all how long eighteen miles would take me with a backpack. I don't recall much of this first day other than worrying about having enough water to last me for the day and being amazed at seeing so many cars with boat trailers. It also struck me as odd to see buses towing cars, motorcycles, wave runners, boats, trailers and whatever else you can possibly think of.

After noticing that half of my little toenail had already departed nonchalantly, I had to make sure there were enough supplies to keep my feet healthy. I needed to stock up on band-aids. At the nearest pharmacy, I was struck by another Florida Keys phenomenon. I noticed a whole section of fishing rods and other fishing gear, taking up what seemed like a quarter of the pharmacy. Fishing was sold as medicine down here!

After exiting the store, I spent some minutes applying band aids all over my feet, which felt strangely re-assuring and comforting. I must have had a premonition of the hammering my feet were about to get. Filling my backpack with water and electrolyte drinks, off I went on the Overseas Highway to Islamorada, one foot in front of the other. My shirt was soaked within the first twenty minutes of walking. Of course, I took cotton shirts, which was a stupid thing to do. As a punishment for my stupidity and not taking moisture-wicking T-shirts, I would be wearing a wet shirt for the remainder of the day, the next day, oh and on all the other days after that.

It was a humid day and the weight strapped to my back slowed me down. However, I got used to it quickly and resigned myself to the fact that this was how it was going to be for the next week. The scenery soon made up for initial hardship and loss of toenails. There was so much beauty all around me. For miles, I saw no humans and no other walkers or cyclists, only cars, trucks, a couple of squirrels and lots of landscape. I noticed wildlife by the side of the road, mainly birds and squirrels, acting strangely. The animals were so used to being exposed to cars but much less to humans. My presence seemed to confuse and scare them much more than a huge truck roaring past.

Crystal clear waters, boats and birds were lining my path. I was constantly looking around me and discovering new things. Crossing my first bridge, I saw boats and wonderful houses on the water, all with their own dockage. What a little paradise. I never remembered seeing all this when driving along the Overseas Highway. I felt so uplifted seeing this beauty, it was truly magical. I remember thinking: "this is going to be hard, but maybe I can do it - just maybe." I was not sure whether I would be able to finish the walk successfully but at least I was rewarded with beautiful scenery at almost every step.

Interestingly, I could also feel my mind slowly clearing of the negative and dark thoughts that had ruled over me in the weeks prior to the walk. While I was concentrating on putting one foot in front of the other and looking around me, my mind started to recalibrate.

I had lost my job? Well, I would find a new one. I had to move continents? I moved continents before. I had to give up my condo on the ocean? I could try to find another nice place somewhere close to the ocean. Suddenly, nothing seemed quite as dramatic as it had before. I was alive, healthy and my surroundings were beautiful. I was feeling more appreciative and grateful with every step.

After midday, exhaustion was starting to slow me down. I had walked almost twelve miles before noon and passed the "Islamorada Welcomes You" sign, but the following few miles felt extremely tough. Generally, the heat in the afternoon was stifling. If there was any chance of me making the schedule, I needed to walk the bulk of daily miles before noon.

My feet were another concern. Despite diligently swapping footwear, I had not factored in the extra backpack weight increasing wear and tear on my feet and legs. Further, I had not spared a thought about mosquito bites that would swell up in strategic places, such as the back of the knees and top of feet, adding more pain to the equation and actually slowing me down. Those little blighters!

I was well and truly on my last legs for the day, when I finally spotted the sign for my lodgings in Islamorada. I had been staring at my GPS every hundred feet or so for the last two miles. The last mile seemed to stretch into infinity. When I finally checked in at the motel and got into my room, I shrugged off my backpack and collapsed onto the bed with outstretched legs. Then, like a parched woman who had just found an oasis in the desert, I gulped down a huge amount of water mixed with a sugary vending-machine drink, for some added energy.

It took me a while to haul myself off the bed again, but eventually I had a nice hot shower and began to think about food. I was half dead after these eighteen miles, and it occurred to me that this week-long walk was going to be a tall order. Could I even finish it? I honestly didn't know. Doubts began to rear their ugly head yet again; I was dreading the next day. Feeling a little restored but still sore after the shower, I walked around a little and found the most beautiful area oceanside with a bar and grill. Perfect.

After "carb loading" with help of an Islamorada firecracker ale and a good solid meal, my mind and body felt a little soothed. I decided to explore the area around the bar and promptly stumbled over a couple of curious raccoons underfoot. I sat down on the edge of the water for a while alone with my thoughts, watching the sun go down and little fish jump out of the water. I suddenly remembered what led me on this adventure. I was looking for quiet inward reflection, immersing myself in nature and finding inspiration. I had almost forgotten this, with all the worrying about whether I would be able to stick to my schedule. The idyllic evening thankfully made me forget all my doubts for the night and the nineteen mile day that lay ahead.

17. Day 2: Islamorada to Long Key Via Matecumbe Key, Fiesta Key And Long Key State Park (19 Miles)

I set off early. Eager to get on the road, I bypassed my beloved cup of coffee for the second morning. There was proof that if you set your mind to it, almost anything is possible, including survival without a morning coffee. I felt temporarily cured from my only addiction, caffeine.

This was the first nineteen mile day I was ever going to walk, and certainly a first with a big backpack, in high humidity and with aching legs and feet. I set off on my not quite so "merry" way, pondering on how the day was going to turn out.

A couple of miles into my walk, a white pick-up truck suddenly hit the breaks right in front of me. A middle aged man got out and stepped into my path. I sighed, realizing he wanted to make conversation. He introduced himself as "Ken", and it transpired that he was driving the Overseas Highway every day, and had spotted me the day before.

He was wondering whether I was in training for something, the Appalachian Mountain trail perhaps? Did I know that the Appalachian trail was over 2000 miles long? Of course he had never thought about walking all of it, so he explained, but maybe some sections. Although, he went on to say, his knee would not be up to it and he was going to need a knee replacement first.

I told him about my intent to hike down to Key West, just for fun, and was not "in training" for anything. He seemed a little disappointed, maybe expecting a better story. Ken wished me good luck and said he would probably see me the next day too. I smiled, waved good bye and pressed on, thinking it was actually nice to have had a little chat by the side of the road.

It wasn't only Ken that had spotted me walking alongside the road. From day 2 onwards, van and truck drivers (presumably from

67

local businesses), started to honk at me. The last couple of days of my walk I got a lot of honking. Unfortunately, I am pretty confident that this horn honking was not due to my "sexiness" on the road increasing. Quite to the contrary, I was looking increasingly disheveled the further south I got. The Florida Keys are a small community and I am sure some locals saw me every morning on their drive to work, especially if they were traveling down to Key West from one of the upper or middle Keys.

Labor Day Hurricane Of 1935 - Monument In Islamorada

On this day, at Mile Marker 82 Islamorada, I passed the monument for the victims of the Labor Day Hurricane of 1935, one of the worst in US history. It made landfall near Islamorada on Monday, 2nd September 1935 as a category 5 Hurricane with sustained winds of up to 200 miles per hour, and a storm surge of over 17.5 feet (5.3 meters). There would have been little warning. This hurricane undoubtedly caused sheer destruction and horror, washing away man, beast and property like it was all nothing, annihilating everything in its path. There was nowhere to run or hide with the low-lying Florida Keys rising at best a few feet above sea level. More than 400 people were reportedly killed, although some historians place that number at over 600. Many of the victims were US Army veterans housed in tent-like structures on Matecumbe Key, who had come to The Florida Keys as workers, building the Overseas Highway.

The Labor Day Hurricane, as well as causing much human loss, also severed all transportation links, making many parts of The Florida Keys inaccessible by rail, road or ferry boats.

At the time, the Florida East Coast Railway was the primary route to and through The Keys. The above mentioned US Army veterans were working on what is now U.S. 1, the Overseas Highway in The Florida Keys. As the storm strengthened, a train was sent to evacuate veterans and residents. Tragically, the rescue train arrived just as the hurricane reached its peak strength. A tidal wave washed away the train, knocking all but the locomotive off the tracks. Many people drowned trapped inside the rail carriages. The overseas railroad was so heavily damaged by the storm that just a couple of decades after its inauguration in 1912, it was abandoned and never rebuilt.

Ernest Hemingway, who had been sitting out the storm in his Key West home, devoted a whole publication to the Hurricane and the plight of the veterans working on the road construction site. He traveled up to Islamorada only two days after the storm to see the destruction with his own eyes. Hemingway was touched and angered by what he saw and made snide comments about the government's lack of care regarding the veterans. He argued the evacuation train could have been sent earlier, as soon as the hurricane warning was issued. In his publication, he questions the motives of the government in sending the veterans to build a road in the main hurricane season months and housing them in tents.

When reading Hemingway's words from this publication, it is easy to imagine the horror of these poor men, cowering in the low lying mangroves and being washed away by the huge tidal wave, or hit by flying debris, on the very stretch of land that I was walking on:

"The railroad embankment was gone and the men who had cowered behind it and finally, when the water came, clung to the rails, were all gone with it. You could find them face down and face up in the mangroves. The biggest bunch of the dead were in the tangled, always green but now brown, mangroves behind the tanks cars and the water towers. They hung on there, in shelter, until the wind and the rising water carried them away."(Who Murdered the Vets?: A First-Hand Report on the Florida Hurricane, September 17, 1935).

To this day, evacuation of The Florida Keys in the event of a hurricane continues to challenge the authorities of Monroe County and South Florida. This is true even when considering that modern transport and meteorological accuracy are much improved, resulting in more time to prepare an evacuation.

This day was neither an easy day mentally nor was it easy physically. I could feel every mile, especially the last few. My body was telling me, in no uncertain terms, that this was not fair and I worried about getting dehydrated. I took care to mix water with electrolytes and bought little packets of salty nuts whenever I got the chance, to try and satisfy my constant craving for salty foods.

I stopped for lunch for the first time "properly", for a rest longer than ten minutes, at Crazy Billy's in Islamorada. There, I devoured the biggest tuna salad sandwich ever known to man, or to woman in this case. I also covered up my poor feet with more band-aids. I had some pain, which was to be expected, but figured as long as there were no blood blisters or open wounds, all should be fine.

Just as I was starting to relax, I looked down to see hundreds of tiny ants intent on climbing up my legs. The sandwich crumbs liberally strewn all around the ground of the outside picnic area by other lunch customers and yours truly, had turned me into an object of desire. I decided it was time to move on – swiftly. So much for a nice long and relaxing lunch break…

As it happens, people have various needs throughout the day, many of which we don't waste much time thinking about, as they are easily satisfied in everyday life. Not so when you walk by the side of a road all day. The inconvenience of trying to find a convenience can drive you literally potty. In this case, I noticed Crazy Billy's lunch spot disappointingly sporting a plastic "porta-potty" and nothing else in the sanitation department. To make sure, I asked. The guy behind the counter emotionlessly pointed to the porta-potty outside: "the restrooms are there." Ugh.

The problem I have with these types of "conveniences" is that when you open the door, you never quite know what will look at you from the big and dark hole. The hole, sometimes deep and mysterious, is at other times alarmingly shallow and not so mysteriously displaying some of its contents. I spare you from going into more details. There was "no way Jose" I would frequent a plastic cubicle that had been standing in full Florida sunlight and humidity all day long, festering away inclusive of its contents.

Many years of digging in the field as an archaeologist have psychologically scarred me. I have memories – not fond ones – of opening a porta-potty door in an extremely hot European summer, and flies rushing past me to get out of the door, like little ricocheting bullets. It was there I concluded: if flies are unable to tolerate this environment, humans should not even try. Now you know why I avoid the humble porta-potty at all cost.

I sucked it up and walked cross legged, figuratively speaking, for a couple of miles. The area was too populated and busy to consider anything else. Thankfully, relief finally came in form of a marina. I bought the obligatory bottle of water (spot the irony) and asked for the restroom. Oh how nice, clean and cool it was. Then my eyes spotted a big sign: "push here to flush". The writing was in huge bold print, framed in bright colors. I immediately started to think of the poor toilet cleaning lady/man and how desperate they would have to be, to point out the blatantly obvious…

As I continued to trudge along without shade and with much heat and humidity accompanying me in the mid-afternoon, a comical

72

scene unfolded on the path ahead of me. In the middle of nowhere on a bland and grassy stretch on Long Key, I heard sirens.

Then I saw the blue and red lights.

Had I done something wrong? Were they here for me? Maybe it was unlawful to walk along the main road? All those thoughts were rushing through my mind.

As I got closer, I saw a few state trooper cars and a van full of what looked like Chinese citizens. To be precise, the van was empty as all the Chinese were standing outside of the van looking glum. The police officers stood next to the group seeming very busy. As far as I was concerned, they were all a nuisance and in my way. I decided to plough right through this group.

It was the second half of the day, I was exhausted and could not waste an inch of concrete to make my way around this strange scene. I just paraded through with firm steps and a courteous "hello", reasoning that common courtesy must always be observed. Apparently, nobody else was keen on common courtesy, no one answered back, which immediately got me a little annoyed. I wanted to tell them that being polite costs nothing. They all just stared at me, the Chinese and the cops, as if I was some type of exotic animal. Worse, after I had said my cheerful greeting, one cop actually put his hand on his gun holster. Perhaps it was just a coincidence but it made me shake my head as I walked on unfazed, wondering why anyone would be scared of me.

A little further along the road, I came across a small convenience store. I walked in for a breath of fresh air-conditioning and a cold soda, a total luxury on lonely stretches of road when cold drinks were hard to come by. The shop owner's dog on seeing me, went absolutely berserk and would not stop barking. I thought the poor thing was going to wear itself out. Nothing helped, not my kind words or indeed the owner-lady's kind words, petting and reassurance. I paid quickly, clutched my cold drink and hurried out of there.

With only a couple of miles to go I should have been happy at this point, but facing the full sun and afternoon heat reflecting from the asphalt, I was cursing. Why on earth had I not taken a hat? Finally, after a slight GPS confusion resulting in a big panic, thinking I might have to walk miles further, I arrived at Edgewater Lodge. I felt annihilated and probably looked like having been dragged through a bush backwards - several times. Then I heard someone call my name as I limped pathetically into the courtyard: "Tamara, are you Tamara?" Of course I was instantly recognizable. Only a severely visually impaired person could have mistaken me for a sane vacationer or a local. I looked like a dirty, sweaty tramp with craziness in my eyes. Of course I didn't quite realize how bad it really was, until I got spooked by a glimpse of my own reflection in the bathroom mirror later on.

It felt so nice being greeted by the friendly Cynthia at Edgewater Lodge, despite the way I must have looked and perhaps even smelled? Sweet Cynthia showed me to my wonderful room, directly at the waterfront, and just as I thought I was in paradise, she shocked me with the sentence: "No, there is nowhere to get food around here in walking distance". Oh no. I put on a brave face, when all I wanted to do was cry like a baby. No food?

I had walked almost twenty miles and now a huge hole in my stomach. All I had was a large packet of nuts. I was about to go through the full five stages of a breakup, namely the breakup with my prospect of a warm meal: denial, anger, bargaining, depression and finally acceptance. First denial then anger set in - I wanted to cry and throw a tantrum but remained composed. I proceeded straight to "bargaining", mumbling to myself: "it's not over until the fat lady sings." I grabbed my phone and dialed every restaurant within a twenty mile radius that offered delivery, only to be told: "Long Key? No, we certainly don't deliver there." After half an hour, the fat lady sang.

Then stage four: depression set in as I pulled out what remained of my provisions. Eventually, acceptance, as I let go of the hope for a warm meal once and for all and opened up my packet of nuts. Defeat! I tried to enjoy my nuts washed down with lashings of tepid tap water. After a nineteen mile day walking, I ate the whole giant packet, briefly remembering a story about almonds containing an acid that can cause poisoning when eating too many at once. I was past caring. As I threw one handful of almonds after another into my mouth, I decided to enjoy the wonderful sunset and wildlife in front of me that evening. This day was a good lesson in being grateful and enjoying what is. Even when dinner is just a bag of nuts.

18. Day 3: Long Key To Marathon Via Duck Key, Crawl Key And Fat Deer Key (15 Miles)

I had high hopes for this day, really looking forward to "only" fifteen miles. It was to be the second shortest distance day of the whole week and felt like having a rest day. In the end it turned out quite a challenging one, at least for the first two hours of walking.

I had woken up with a very bad pain in my right knee, a combination of over overuse and an infected mosquito bite. The mosquito bite had swollen up to the size of an egg and it was in the bend of the knee, so I could not straighten out my leg properly - not without howling from pain in any case. I started off the day with a limp and great deal of pain. This had me worried and wondering how I would be able to walk fifteen miles with a swollen and sore leg. Mostly, I was worried about what caused this bad reaction to the bite and whether I would need to find medical attention for an infection and possibly have to abandon or delay my walk.

As if the painful leg wasn't enough of a challenge, I discovered rashes on my body, particularly on my ankles. They looked like hives, possibly triggered by dirt and scrapes, or pesticides and insect bites from walking in grass next to the road. I also had rashes and sores on my torso from the backpack and perspiration creating friction. After careful inspection of my body, I concluded that I was falling apart. I began to wonder whom of my friends I could call to pick me up just in case things went from bad to worse. However, after a few minutes of feeling sorry for myself, I decided to ignore it all and just carry on walking one step in front of the other, pain and limp or not.

I had to cross a sizeable bridge called the "Long Key Viaduct". Unlike many of the other bridges, I was lucky to avoid traffic thanks to this pedestrian bridge running alongside the motorized bridge, courtesy of the Florida Keys Overseas Heritage Trail. The weather was amazing, a lovely morning with blue skies.

The first person I met on the bridge was a very friendly man. He was fishing off the bridge and had a nice little collection of fish already, this early on in the day. I asked if I could watch a little. He was happy to show me what he had just caught and said he had about twenty five fish biting already today, in just one hour. As if to prove what he had said, his rod was promptly bending: fish on! He tossed that one back in, it was too small to keep. As soon as he put the line back into the water, yet another fish was pulling on it. I couldn't believe how full of fish the waters were. It is true that every time I looked into the water, I saw all kinds of fish. No wonder The Florida Keys are such a well-known fishing destination. I also noticed that it was possible to get bait and tackle literally on every corner, unlike food and drink – much to my dismay. Maybe I should have taken a fishing rod and caught my own food along the way?

Sadly, the nice man and I had to part ways after a few minutes, as I was on a schedule. However, he was not going to let me go before rummaging in his bag, and pulling out a handful of band aids, saying: "I am sure these will come in handy". He went on to say that he would happily give me a fish for dinner, but as that was not really an option, band-aids would have to suffice. This lovely man was just one example of the many nice people I met in The Florida Keys, another wonderful facet of the walk. It really made me so very happy to meet good-natured and sweet people along the way, most with just as much enthusiasm for nature and wildlife as me.

It was time to carry on along the bridge which seemed never-ending and yet was only the beginning of my day's walk. Suddenly, I had a very human need. One of the challenges of walking The Florida Keys is that quite often one is pretty much exposed – no pun intended – to traffic and there simply isn't the option to "pee in a bush". Sometimes, it is possible to tread through a little shrubbery to hide behind, by the side of the road. Other times, the road turns into a narrow strip with small single bushes and mangroves, none of them thick enough to hide behind, or more specifically: to hide your behind behind. You get the picture. It's not always easy to find relief. Plus, well, there are snakes in the grass.

The day ended on a couple of pleasant and funny notes. I passed yet another bridge with another fisherman who saw me limping and stopping to apply band-aids to my aching feet. He started talking to me, asking what I was doing. After a little chit-chat, he lowered his voice and whispered: "I can give you something for the road, if you know what I mean." Despite the heat and advanced hours, the penny dropped quickly. I informed him that I was more of an "umbrella drinks" kind of girl and swiftly departed, thinking the last thing I needed was getting into trouble, because some guy had pockets full of weed to hand out. Gathering speed, I quickly put some distance between me and weed man.

Just two miles before my lodgings, I met the next character: Davey from Marathon. He stopped his truck in the middle of the road and shouted "can I take you to the bus station or something". After all, he had "just gotten his driver's license back". Ah! Tempting as it was (not), I decided to pass on his kind offer. "Besides", I explained to him, "I am walking on purpose. I am walking the whole of The Florida Keys". After a little silence he said: "Ok. Hm. What about fishing?" Now he had the right kind of bait! I never normally miss an invitation for boating. I explained that I was on a tight schedule, sadly. He handed me a saltwater bleached and frayed business card with his details, and said it was an "anytime kinda deal". As I bid him goodbye, I was wondering whether he was a better captain than driver.

For once I had made it to my lodgings at a decent early afternoon hour, around 3pm, and was able to enjoy the luxury of a motel pool. Joy of joys! It felt like heaven to have the time to unwind and float in the pool for a few minutes and give my aching limbs some gentle relief. I did ponder on how much more enjoyable this walk might have been, had I planned on shorter days, up to fifteen miles per day perhaps. Oh well, Shakespeare always offers some wisdom for such idle thoughts: "what's done can't be undone."

The negative thoughts of the weeks prior had by this point all but disappeared. I was enjoying the remainder of the walk with newly found enthusiasm for my life and the future. If I could manage this walk, I could manage any other challenges that would undoubtedly present themselves in the weeks ahead.

After floating weightlessly in the pool for a while, I set off for a well earned meal. Remember, I had literally only eaten peanuts, well almonds, the night before. It felt so right to make the only hot meal I had in twenty four hours one humungous burger, and yes, I definitely wanted fries with that. After my meal, I felt no longer famished but rather relaxed and started to observe life around me, "life in Marathon", as it were.

It transpired quickly that the people at this bar all knew each other. I witnessed several customers walking in and out of the bar area, fetching their own beverages from the fridge, while the waitress was pottering around elsewhere and paid little attention. I briefly wondered what would happen if I tried that? I didn't try but I should have, for research purposes only of course.

One customer gave the waitress' little daughter a ride home after school. The girl had been hanging about at the bar, drawing little pictures and talking to people. She obviously felt comfortable there and everybody knew her. It made me smile to see such a trusting and caring community and I wondered how it would be living here in

Marathon. Alas, I could not stay for long. I needed rest and sleep for the next leg of the walk.

How Did Marathon Get Its Name?

Marathon is a fairly recently designated city (since 1999). It comprises: Knight's Key, Boot Key, Key Vaca, Fat Deer Key, Long Point Key, Crawl Key and Grassy Key in the middle Keys. As of the census in the year 2000, Marathon has over ten thousand residents (10.255, https://en.wikipedia.org/wiki/Marathon,_Florida).

An interesting story circulates about how Marathon got its fairly recent name. Before the extension of the East Coast Railway route, the area went by various names, for example Key Vaca, Port Monroe and Conch Town. The arrival of the railroad caused the re-naming of many places in The Florida Keys, as they became identified with the new railroad station names. Marathon was one of those renamed places.

Why "Marathon"? Well, the story goes that by the middle Keys, the workers building on the railroad exclaimed: "What is this, a marathon?" and "This is getting to be a real marathon".

The workers must have realized just how much they still had to toil to reach Key West, including building the famous 7 Mile Bridge. It was decided to name the railroad station "Marathon", and as with other communities in The Florida Keys, the station name soon became synonymous with the area and was adopted as the name henceforth (www.keyshistory.org).

Nowadays, Marathon is one of the larger communities in The Florida Keys and famous for deep sea, reef and flats fishing, as well as all kinds of water sports. Marathon is also home to the Dolphin Research Center, Turtle Hospital and a couple of State Parks: Crane Point Hammock and Curry Hammock State Park. Going south upon leaving Marathon, there is also historic Pigeon Key accessible via the Old 7 Mile Bridge and definitely worth a visit.

19. Day 4: Marathon To Big Pine Key Via 7 Mile Bridge And Bahia Honda Key (20 Miles)

Today was the much dreaded twenty mile day. I set off very early, at 7am, knowing what lay ahead of me: twenty exhausting long miles, including the 7 Mile Bridge. I had awaited the bridge with some trepidation after having heard from a previous walker that it could get quite hairy, and that there was nowhere to stop on the bridge.

Unfortunately, with the early start came a much bigger dose of the daily plague of hungry mosquitos. I was practically chased down the road by the bloodsuckers. This swarming of my person induced some mad arm flailing and swatting, which must have looked pretty amusing to the many cars passing me with people driving to work.

On a side note, nothing helped against those little blood suckers. I seemed to be the equivalent of lobster and champagne for the common Keys mosquito. If you are not a mosquito magnet, you might have a different experience. However, in my case, mosquitos were not deterred by long sleeved garments (stinging right through), or by mosquito repellant. It confused them for a while, but they always found a place to land and sting: feet, fingers, neck, backside, you name it. I often had to think of the early settlers and pioneers exploring Florida in the days before aerial mosquito spraying and mosquito repellant. Not to forget they didn't have air-conditioning and refrigeration either. I really wanted to take my hat off and would have, had I taken one.

Undoubtedly, the bugs, swamp and almost unbearable heat were some of the reasons as to why Florida was settled relatively late in the history of the US. I also shudder when I remember reading about the workers on the overseas railroad in the 1930's, having to rake mosquitos off their arms and breathing them in. Eyewitness accounts speak of swarms as thick as clouds!

This day was one of my most amazing as well as most frustrating days. After I ran from the mosquitos, I decided today would be the day for a much needed caffeine boost. The early start had left me craving for a coffee. When I came across a gas station advertising "fresh coffee", I wasted no time and traipsed inside. Not sure whether I was still half asleep or whether the mosquitos had robbed my last nerve, but what happened then had the potential to send me straight to a mental institution.

Coffee in hand, I opened a little plastic cream packet and absentmindedly poured the contents (the cream) into the trash can, whilst throwing the empty packet into my coffee cup. It made a "plop" sound and floated like a tiny defiant lopsided ship on top of a black coffee ocean. I watched it for a few seconds until the penny dropped. Looking around nervously, I hoped nobody had witnessed this scene. Of course, I wasn't so lucky. A man had silently watched me, and with a look of pity asked: "are you ok, Miss?"

I quickly paid and tried to escape from the scene of embarrassment with my (black) coffee and a banana, walking back outside into mosquito territory. There, I stood in relative peace with my goods, content that at least I hadn't thrown away my banana and tried to eat the peel. Although I had the peace of no longer being watched by people, I was now mosquito breakfast again. Then a man walked past, giving me a stare as though I was some kind of zoo animal. Worse, he then started to laugh, symbolically holding his stomach. He was mocking me!

Enough was enough. I was ready to cry like a baby. Someone poking fun at you can feel a little demoralizing when you are at your best. Ordinarily, I might have laughed this little episode off. However, I was tired, worried that I might not make my schedule, my limbs hurt, I had just been chased and stung by a gazillion mosquitos, and last but by no means least had thrown an empty creamer packet into my coffee. Making fun of me at this point was just adding insult to injury. It was almost as bad as having to drink black coffee.

I was first feeling emotional and then angry, but quickly consoled myself with vowing to use the f-word on him, yes the F-

WORD, should he ever cross my path again. I had been pushed over the edge and I would let him know. Of course, I never saw the stomach-holding guy again and never got the satisfaction of throwing the "f-word" his way.

I generally got a wonderful reception from The Florida Keys community, but there were a few instances when I was met by outright hostility and rudeness. The above example was one of them. In general, it seemed to me that the hostility did not come from locals, rather workers who were perhaps seasonal. There was another example of this that caused my blood to boil.

I asked a lady at a vacation village where I could buy water. She was standing in front of a soda vending machine, barely inside of their yard, I could clearly see it from the sidewalk. While I explained to her that I had just walked ten miles and had more to go, I was already fishing for coins from my pocket, thinking this was a total no-brainer. Then, the unthinkable happened: I saw her close the gate in front of me. She told me with a gravely serious face: "keep walking south, it's very close."

She must have seen my tongue hanging to the floor. I was shocked. Even worse, her "very close" turned out to be about another two miles away. Two miles down the road for a walker carrying a backpack, sweaty and thirsty in the midday heat, is quite a long way - almost another hour. I had the feeling that I might as well have collapsed there and then, in the heat and full sun, without getting any kind help or reaction from this lady. Always making a point of being polite and pleasant to everybody, I felt disappointed.

Today, Marathon was not going to be kind to me either. Just before the 7 Mile Bridge, I was accused of stealing. I had made a pit stop before the bridge to get some essentials, as I knew there would be miles without any stores or civilization to come. I had water but needed some snacks and decided to stop at the last gas station before the bridge, not thinking much about having a half empty water bottle peeking out of the top of my backpack.

Walking in through the door and not wanting to waste time, I grabbed a couple of bags of nuts and made a beeline for the check out. Suddenly, the cashier started wildly gesticulating in my general direction. It seemed quite entertaining, not knowing what had brought it on. I looked behind me, but strangely there was nobody. She didn't speak a syllable of English and I had absolutely no idea what she was going on about, but it slowly started to dawn on me that this wild gesticulating and spewing out of many words in the Spanish tongue, was actually directed at me.

The cashier lady, huffing and puffing, walked off to get one of the other assistants to translate. I realized then that this was unlikely to be friendly small talk. The assistant informed me that, apparently, I had just stolen a bottle of water from their fridge, insinuating that I had somehow contorted myself to stick this bottle of water into my backpack (which had been resting on my shoulders the entire two minutes I had spent in the store). Quite a ridiculous suggestion, considering the water in my backpack was clearly half empty and warm. It wouldn't have taken the brains of a rocket scientist to work out that it didn't come from their fridge. I was incensed!

Nobody had ever accused me of stealing anything at all. Not even as a child had I as much as taken a piece of candy without paying for it. By pure chance, thank God, I still had the receipt of the purchase from earlier in the day, but I was pretty shocked and disappointed. I held up the receipt triumphantly and mumbled a few swear words as I walked out.

Putting two and two together, I can only assume carrying a backpack and wearing walking shoes aroused general suspicion amongst some members of society. Maybe they thought I was homeless or had fallen on hard times? Still, I felt pretty deflated and angry. This was one of the very few occasions where I felt misunderstood and discriminated against, simply because I was backpacking. Luckily this was a rare event on my walk and happened only those times I recounted above. Most of the other people I met out and about whilst walking or in stores and restaurants, were curious, encouraging, friendly and sweet.

Eventually, not much after the gas station water bottle "debacle", I arrived at the start of the 7 Mile Bridge. I took a deep breath and began to walk. It was impossible for me to see land on the other side, only what seemed like a never-ending bridge with an elevation in the middle. In hindsight, I need not have worried. Yes, it was tough and yes, there was a lot of heavy traffic rolling on and off the bridge, but walking it turned out to be a very magical and exhilarating experience. I might even go as far as to call walking the 7 Mile Bridge the highlight of the whole trip.

The overwhelming majority of drivers were extremely courteous and made a wide berth around me when they could, so all the worrying about traffic beforehand was largely unwarranted. There were some exceptions, let's call them "swervers". Some cars and trucks would swerve towards me, only to make a fast pull away, sometimes ending up in the opposite traffic lane, which was somewhat alarming. It is apparently common to subconsciously steer towards an object or a person in sight whilst driving. Who knew?

Whether walking or driving this route, you will notice two bridges at the start of the 7 Mile Bridge. The older and somewhat dilapidated 7 Mile Bridge will be on your right hand side as you travel south on the Overseas Highway. There will most likely be people walking on the old bridge (no vehicular traffic). You might start to wonder what the heck you are doing, facing all this traffic whilst all those people look so happy strolling along the car-free old bridge on the other side. Then suddenly, as you get further towards Pigeon Key, the explanation presents itself by way of a gaping hole in the old bridge. So do not get tempted to walk the old 7 Mile Bridge, unless you are planning on spending an extra day in Marathon with a little excursion to Pigeon Key. The old bridge is a dead-end.

The exit ramp leading to Pigeon Key is also clearly visible when walking the new 7 Mile Bridge. The old bridge is in fact part of the Florida Keys Overseas Heritage Trail and accessible up to, and including, historic Pigeon Key. Sadly, I did not have time to walk it and stop there.

A Little History Of The 7 Mile Bridge

The old 7 Mile Bridge was constructed in 1909 as a railroad bridge initially, part of Henry Flagler's Overseas Railroad. The construction of the bridge was an engineering feat, and certainly an extremely challenging one. Steel-girder spans, weighing no less than nineteen tons each, were supported on concrete foundation piers which in turn were secured to bedrock. The bedrock foundations were sometimes as much as twenty eight feet below the waterline.

The old 7 Mile Bridge took four years to complete. Sadly, it sustained a great deal of damage from the Labor Day Hurricane of 1935. After the hurricane, the railway line was sold to the US government. Federal government subsequently refurbished the 7 Mile Bridge for car use, a sign of the times. It had a swing span that opened to allow boat traffic. You can see where the old swing bridge was located, which is now a big gap. Hurricane Donna (1960) caused further damage to the bridge. The old 7 Mile Bridge was once referred to as the "8th Wonder of the World".

The current 7 Mile Bridge was constructed from 1978 to 1982. The vast majority of the original bridge still exists and is used as a fishing pier, for walking and as access to historic Pigeon Key. The total length of the new bridge is only 6.79 miles. It is therefore shorter than the original. You can find more information on the old 7 Mile Bridge at the "Friends Of Old Seven" website: www.friendsofoldseven.org.

Further along on the 7 Mile Bridge, I saw the most amazing wildlife, including a green sea turtle popping her little head out of the dark blue waters. I could also see a lot of jellyfish, which the turtle would have been feeding on. There were plenty of fish and birds. At some point during the walk, I decided that rather than listen to noisy car traffic, I was going to listen to music. It was perhaps not the wisest thing to do, rendering the traffic inaudible, but it helped me to keep a good pace. I "conquered" the bridge pretty quickly in just over two hours. Considering the backpack and struggling with a very windy day, particularly at the highest point of the bridge, two hours made for a fast walking time.

Then came the really tough part: carrying on for another ten miles at the other end of the 7 Mile Bridge. I had virtually no shade all day and suddenly my feet and blisters started to make themselves known. However, the unbelievably amazing scenery at the other side of the 7 Mile Bridge soon made up for all the aches and pains, at least temporarily. Alongside the old Bahia Honda Bridge, another Flagler engineering marvel, the water looked particularly mesmerizing and inviting in all shades of turquoise. Pelicans flew in formation overhead. I spotted some dolphins hunting in the distance. Boats with happy people onboard rushed through the channels. I felt so incredibly humbled and uplifted by all this beauty. It inspired me to bite the bullet, feel the pain and carry on regardless. My philosophy of "one foot in front of the other" saw me through yet another day.

On the new Bahia Honda Bridge, with still a good few miles to go, I was stopped by Mike from Kentucky. Apparently, he had seen me walking for the second consecutive day already and wanted to talk to me. Mike had grabbed his bike and followed me until he caught up. He was staying at an RV park in Bahia Honda and much like me, Mike was fascinated by this beautiful part of the world. We walked the path for maybe half a mile together and had a very pleasant conversation. Mike kindly invited me out for dinner that evening but I still had so many miles to go and could not even think about the evening. I just knew I would be way too tired later on, so I had to decline.

Eventually, after what seemed like an eternity of passing a sea of mangroves, I saw Big Pine Key, part of the National Key Deer Refuge area and home of the famous Key Deer. Walking into the center of Big Pine Key, exhausted but happy, on the left a church with a pumpkin patch attracted my attention. I remembered that it was Halloween. Needing to sit down for a little moment, after having hardly stopped all day for fear of not making it to my lodgings before darkness, I walked towards the pumpkins. There had only been a hasty ten minute lunch stop at Veterans Park right after the 7 Mile Bridge and I needed to catch my breath.

At the pumpkin patch, I was greeted by a lovely man, Jim, who was the guardian of the pumpkins. He kindly handed me a bottle of cold water whilst introducing himself to me. There, I also saw my first two Key Deer. They are cute and perfect little creatures with big eyes and really quite tame. I got very excited at seeing them. Jim and I started talking and time passed, but half an hour later I had to force myself to carry on walking. I still had a little way to go and could feel my legs seizing up.

Jim invited me to his and his wife's house for dinner and again I felt sad not to be able to accept. I instinctively knew that I wouldn't be able to face stepping out of my motel room again, once arriving there after this long and hot twenty mile day. It had been one of the longest and toughest days of the week, but also one of the most rewarding. The scenery, the achievement and meeting such lovely people all contributed to making this one of the most memorable days of the walk.

Finally, I made it to the motel. As soon as I walked over the threshold, I was greeted with the words: "oh you must be Tamara the walker, right?" I was laughing, because yes, I guess it was quite obvious. Unfortunately, I had caught my reflection in the glass door (not recommended), and started to frantically pat down my humidity-crazed hair. It didn't help much. I looked like a hot mess altogether.

Oh, yet again the sweet disappointment of having arrived in civilization but unable to find a place to eat close by. I took the motel lady's advice, after asking her where to eat, and "ordered in". Something I had not factored in whilst planning for the walk was having close availability of food sources near my lodgings. I was very lucky, and only once did I end up with nothing close by, but twice my poor feet had to carry me another mile or two in the hunt for something to eat. At the end of a twenty mile day, the very last thing I wanted to do today was to walk yet more.

Luckily, I was all set up for a nice delivery in Big Pine Key. However, it occurred to me that it would be a great treat to whet my whistle with something other than tepid tap water from the motel bathroom tap. The prospect of a cold adult beverage did wonders for my motivation. On that promise, my feet somehow carried me to a liquor store just across the road from the motel. There, I saw something I had never seen before: a "drive-through" liquor store. I curiously observed a customer drive up to the little window and saw the liquor store man poke his head out. Guess what happened then? They talked and talked and talked and talked some more. This served as a timely reminder for me, with my tendency to impatience: I was in The Florida Keys and still on island time. Who was in a rush anyway? Not me...

This scenario, however, left me wondering what the point was of having a drive-through liquor store. Surely it couldn't be to save time with all the chatting going on through that window. They must have talked for at least ten minutes while I was inside.

Then came my turn to have a good old chat, I mean: my turn to purchase a drink. The owner started talking to me, which was very welcome after a day of mostly solitary walking. I understood then that the daily chat and small talk was inclusive of the liquor purchase and considered customer service. He told me a little about the history of Big Pine Key, how he ended up there as a transplant, and of course about liquor stores. In the olden days, apparently, it was common to see drive-through bars here, where you could grab an alcoholic beverage right from your driver's seat. Just wind down the window, grab your drink and off you go "drink driving" - literally. Although glad that times have changed, this amused me greatly.

20. Day 5: Big Pine Key To Sugarloaf Key Via Little Torch Key, Summerland Key And Cudjoe Key (14 Miles)

On this day, I woke up to a beautiful thought: only fourteen miles to walk. I had a nice lie-in and decided to start around 8:30, pretty late for me. I was hoping the majority of my buzzing, blood-sucking friends had already embarked on their daytime sleep.

Incidentally, where do mosquitos go in the majority of the daytime? Although they are awake all day in the summertime in mangrove areas, including in The Florida Keys, most only show up in the dusk and dawn hours – why? Well, most mosquito species rest or sleep in a dark and humid place during the day. Apparently, mosquitos get dehydrated quickly by sunlight during the daytime hours, so they try to avoid daytime and the sun, just like Count

Dracula.

I was almost deliriously happy on realizing: no mosquitos today. It was a mosquito-free morning, hurrah! The happiness didn't last all that long, because here entered the stage (drumroll): no-see-ums. I was now getting bitten by a new to me species the locals called "no-see-ums". The name makes sense as they are very tiny and you really can't see 'um until you feel the bite. They are so minute, yet their bites are nasty and persistent, leaving little itchy bumps lasting up to ten days. Ten days? Give me mosquitos any day.

This was the morning I finally relaxed into believing I would finish this walk. I started to feel confident rather than worried about not being able to make it for whatever reason. The worry of not being able to keep up with my schedule or having to abandon the walk, had been a constant companion during the first few days. Suddenly, the worry about failure disappeared. Not only was I now convinced I could finish, but also after today there would be only one more day left to walk. I could see light at the end of the tunnel and for a change it didn't appear to be an oncoming train.

I was feeling a little proud of myself and confident on my penultimate walking day. This was the first time I had felt proud of myself for quite some time, possibly the whole year. At the same time, ironically, I felt a little sad that this adventure was nearly over. My feet and legs were pretty beaten up and I was in pain, but I was now used to my routine of walk, eat, sleep and starting it all over again the next day. I enjoyed this simple daily rhythm, where all that was expected of me was physical. My mind was free to observe beauty and wander all day long. The longer it wandered, the more positive I felt. In any case, there wasn't much I could do about the pain and blisters on my feet, so I had learnt to simply tolerate the discomfort rather than fight it. I got surprisingly good at walking with some pain all the time.

The scenery was so breathtaking in the lower Florida Keys, it made my pains and aches seem much less obvious and even unnoticeable during the course of the day. Knowing I could complete the walk and was almost there, gave me new energy and put a spring in my step. For the first time, I was able to fully relax and soak in everything: the beauty of nature, the wildlife and the lovely people I met. My thoughts were predominantly cheerful and positive.

As I was happily walking along the Overseas Highway, I came across a sizeable snake roadkill, which admittedly was a little shock to the system. Yes, I was aware of snakes, and indeed poisonous snakes living here, but when you never see any, they somehow don't exist. Seeing this snake, a harmless rat snake (I later found out), made me think a little next time I jumped into the undergrowth. After the snake encounter, I cut my "walking in undergrowth and peeing behind bushes" time down to the bare minimum.

Another curious thing I came across was a number of fishing lines swinging in the wind, often on power lines over the fishing bridges. Sometimes, this would look quite macabre with bait, often a whole little fish, and tackle still attached. There would be a mess of fishing lines like a spider's web, from which hooks and dead baitfish dangled. I had a hard time imagining how they got there. In the end, I guessed strong gusts whipped the lines up into the sky and onto the power-lines, never to be retrieved again. It is definitely a "Keys thing", as I saw this on quite a few bridges.

There was a lot of walking through fairly remote stretches of the Overseas Highway today, with humidity on the rise. I got tired and hungry and knew after my Long Key food disaster, I should be making a plan. So I enlisted my trusty friend google and found a restaurant right on the Overseas Highway and only three miles before my stopping point for the night. It was called "Mangrove Mama's". That sounded perfect - I simply had to stop there. This little rustic place summed up the whole Florida Keys feeling, all the things I had been dreaming of, before setting off on this walk. The good stuff that never really materialized: tiki bars, umbrella drinks and palm trees swaying in the breeze. Instead up until here it had mainly been blood, sweat, mosquito bites, tears, more sweat and blisters.

Finally, I was on "island time", if only for an hour. I was feeling so relaxed and happy among the bright colors and the decked patio with quirky sea themed decorations. All the people around me were friendly and I was enjoying a good chat with a few, something I really treasured after a day of pounding concrete by myself. The waitress let me try some grouper cheeks, which were sitting temptingly on a plate by the bar. Who'd have known that groupers had such big and tasty cheeks?

I ended up ordering a cracked conch sandwich for the novelty of it, not really knowing what "cracked conch" was. After all, I was almost in the Conch Republic, so it seemed appropriate. The waitress helpfully piped up: "be prepared to chew is all I'm saying". I do love honesty. When the cracked conch arrived, I was almost disappointed as it wasn't very chewy, it was in fact pretty good. This was despite the comment from the waitress having sent my expectations plummeting to expect a shoe sole.

I loved this place, especially the cute bit of inspiration on the bathroom wall of Mangrove Mama's: "beauty lives in the soul." Indeed. Reading this made me feel a whole lot better because I felt anything but beautiful after a day on the road looking grubby, sweaty and crazy-haired. Luckily, my soul was relatively unaffected by superficial appearances.

Back on the road, I had only three miles left to walk. Spurred on by the cracked conch and a good rest, those miles just flew by. Suddenly, I was there. Slap bang in the middle of what looked and felt like paradise: Sugarloaf Key. This was quickly turning into my all-time favorite Key for tranquility and an "Old Keys" feel. To think I almost skipped Sugarloaf when I was planning the walk. However, being very limited as to where I could stop just before getting to Key West without going over my twenty mile daily limit, I was forced to stop and overnight here. Thank goodness.

This is not your usual tourist stop-off or a state of the art resort. There is only one place to stay on Sugarloaf (except for the KOA), a motel called Sugarloaf Lodge. The lodge had certainly seen better days and looked largely unchanged from the 1970s. I loved it nonetheless. I fell in love with Sugarloaf Lodge for many reasons, the most important one: all rooms had a fantastic view, facing out onto the mirror smooth waters of Sugarloaf Bay. The tiki bar attracts plenty of local patronage coming from all directions with their little flats boats in the evenings. Rush hour traffic at Sugarloaf is the humming noise of little motors plowing through the shallows. For me, who had been walking by the side of the dusty and noisy road for days, this tranquility, unspoiled nature and silence was pure heaven.

Sugarloaf Key itself is indeed a quiet paradise. Time seems to have stopped here. At Sugarloaf Lodge's dock, I met a little boy of no more than six years old, who knew all the different fish species. He identified them for me as they swam by, and was eager to show me everything he knew about the life underwater. I could not help thinking how wonderful it would be if all children could grow up like this little boy. He did not need a TV or a phone to play games, he just stood at the dock for hours staring into the water.

After a little rest, it was time for me to explore Sugarloaf Key. I had heard about the historic Bat Tower close to Sugarloaf Lodge, so I took a little walk trying to find it. Suddenly, Lance and his "hound" crossed my path. Lance was probably in his early 30s and looked like Sugarloaf's most eligible bachelor. He sported bare feet, a fraying straw hat and an outrageous tan. His four-legged friend completed this idyllic and somewhat comical picture. Lance informed me of the precise name of breed I was looking at, some hound. I promptly forgot the rest of the breed's name, being too busy taking this picture all in. The hound looked like an oversized dalmatian with droopy eyes and was sporting a boating rope instead of a leash, which he was dragging behind him with the end lying in the dirt road. He did not look intent on escaping, trotting faithfully behind Lance. Together they made quite the team.

Once I had managed to keep a straight face looking at this picture, I asked Lance how he liked living in such a remote place. Lance called Sugarloaf Key his paradise, telling me about his boat and being out on the ocean as much as he could. He described the community to me and being away from cities, and how it all translated to a really good life. After what I had just seen and those few sentences, I understood completely. In fact, I envied him a little with part of me wishing I could swap my life for his. It seemed idyllic, this quiet and simple life on Sugarloaf Key.

The hound, however, trotted on with his head down, seemingly unimpressed by Lance's account, or by my presence for that matter. In the middle of Lance's talk about life on Sugarloaf, and in the middle of the road, the hound started pooping – nonchalantly – all over the road while trudging along as if nothing happened. He did not look up or pause his trot for one moment. I had never seen a dog doing "its business" like that, or indeed a hound, in fact it reminded me of a horse. Maybe it was a horse-hound? Lance was quick to apologize on the hound's behalf: "oh, I apologize for my dog's manners, he just doesn't give a shit anymore since he turned twelve." I swallowed the comment on the tip of my tongue: looks like he does give a s…

As it got gloomy, I decided to turn back to the lodge, thinking how nice it would have been had Lance invited me to a spot of boating. Oh well. Back at Sugarloaf Lodge, I got talking to a nice woman from California. After exchanging some pleasantries, she went on to tell me a story of two women disappearing on Sugarloaf Key. Apparently, a handsome "nice" guy took them boating and they were never to be seen again. I wondered whether it was true? In any case, it made me feel less sad about not receiving a boating invitation. I was dying to find out more about this story, but the poor woman and I were attacked by hundreds of no-see-ums and were scratching without pause, whilst trying to keep up a conversation. This was no fun. I quickly excused myself on account of being exhausted. I didn't fancy scratching all night, no matter how potentially interesting the conversation might have been.

Sugarloaf Key And The Bat Tower

If, like me, you wondered where Sugarloaf Key got its cute name from, apparently there are two theories. One theory suggests the name came from an Indian mound on Upper Sugarloaf Key, which was said to look like an old-fashioned loaf of sugar. The second theory postulates the name's origins stemming from a variety of pineapple called "Sugarloaf", once grown in this area.

Topographically, Sugarloaf is divided into Upper Sugarloaf Key and Lower Sugarloaf Key with most of the population residing on Lower Sugarloaf Key. Despite its smallness and relative close proximity to Key West, Sugarloaf Key has a decent infrastructure, including a school and a little airport.

What about Sugarloaf Key's famous Bat Tower? Perky's Bat Tower is probably the best piece of evidence so far, of me not being the only one driven "batty" by mosquitos in The Keys. I often wondered about the mosquito plague before modern day mosquito control. I found my answer that evening at Sugarloaf Key: the historic Bat Tower. Building a Bat Tower was quite some effort – all that just because the mosquitos were driving people crazy. How bad was it? The Broward Palm Beach New Times reported in the late 19th Century: "swarms so dense in some areas that it was impossible to breathe without inhaling mouthfuls of mosquitos."

Who built this tower? In the 1920s, Richter Clyde Perky, a real estate developer of Denver, planned to establish a fishing resort on

Lower Sugarloaf Key. The construction manager, who was overseeing the project, complained that "in the late afternoon, you would just have to rake the bugs off your arm" and that "they'd form a black print on your hand if you put it against a screen and suck all the blood right out of it" (www.v-e-n-u-e.com/The-Bat-Tower).

No surprise then that Perky felt he needed to take action to protect his future guests. He hired Fred Johnson of Key West, a man who was already helping him with sponging experiments, to build him a tower. The Bat Tower was completed in 1929 and stood thirty feet tall, with four wooden shingled sides of about twelve feet each, all on concrete pillars. Perky reportedly got the plans from Texas, where similar towers had already been constructed for the same reason: mosquito control.

Unfortunately for Perky, the experiment "Perky's Bat Tower" failed, and even after an application of pheromone doused guano as bait, not a single bat ever took up residence in the intricately constructed bat tower. Johnson reportedly said "the smell was awful and we stayed away from there and so did the bats" (www.keyshistory.org). The mosquitos continued to thrive triumphantly in the stagnant waters around the bat tower. Perky's vacation lodge (Perky Lodge), eventually did open - despite mosquitos - in 1939. The Bat Tower still stands now and is just a hop, skip and jump away from the main road, the Overseas Highway, on bayside close to Sugarloaf Lodge.

I couldn't help but reflect on the fact that mosquito control is still such a struggle here in The Keys and in Florida. Nowadays, it takes a full-time team of around seventy employees for Florida Keys Mosquito Control, armed with handheld foggers, spray trucks, four helicopters, and two fixed-wing aircraft, from which they dispense regular doses of larvicide granules and pesticide sprays onto the landscape.

Despite the valiant efforts by The Keys Mosquito Control, my evening at Sugarloaf Key ended in a lot of scratching. The evening also ended with another fairly unspectacular "bag of nuts" dinner. There really was absolutely nowhere to eat in the evening within walking distance, and although I had finally found the tiki bar of my dreams and with it the possibility of the somewhat elusive umbrella drink, I dared not head out there for fear of being eaten alive. The locals seemed immune to swarms of no-see-ums and mosquitos, or perhaps they just didn't care after a few drinks?

21. Day 6: Sugarloaf Key To Key West Mile 0 Via Boca Chica Key And Stock Island (17 Miles)

On my last walking day, I woke up to an amazing morning sky, a wonderful vista and a bunch of little winged visitors at Sugarloaf Lodge. The little birds with long orange beaks - white Ibis - had been a constant feature of my walk. I got used to seeing them most mornings in The Keys, always busily looking for food.

Seventeen miles lay ahead. Just before setting off, disaster struck when I opened my little first aid box: I was almost out of band-aids, again. By then, I had gone through three whole packets of band-aids, plus the handful from the nice fisherman on Long Key Viaduct.

I spent the first hour running from swarms of mosquitos, happily stinging me through my clothes whenever they had the opportunity. After I had lost the mosquitoes, perhaps I was still flailing my arms uncontrollably, I proceeded to spill a – just purchased – hot coffee all over my backpack and me. I thought that this surely had to be the end of all calamities for the day, but no. That last thought had barely left my brain when a screw fell out of my sunglasses. The screw then disappeared into an inexplicable black hole in the Universe, never to be seen again. Goodbye screw and goodbye my favorite sunglasses. This was definitely not my morning.

As soon as I had recovered from the loss of coffee and screw, I looked down on myself with horror: there were coffee stains all over my white linen pants, my T-shirt and the top of my backpack. I went on to try (in vain) to get the coffee stains out of my clothes, briefly wondering whether people might think I was a homeless thief again. Especially with those stained clothes. So I scrubbed like a maniac in the restroom of the gas station where I had purchased the rebellious coffee. All to no avail. I walked out of the place wearing a wet, see-through and stained T-shirt and pants, all sporting fluff from the paper towels I had been using to rub out stains with. Completing the picture was my pair of sunglasses with one arm, now precariously balanced on one ear and my nose. What a mess. On a side note: don't wear white linen pants on a hike, that's just asking for trouble. I should have known.

I felt a little humiliated. Some guy looked at me with pity. I hollered at him "hey, would you mind opening the door for me" still the remnants of (now cold) coffee in cup, arms entangled in two bags. He didn't say a word and continued to stare at me, dutifully opening the door.

From then on the motto of the day would be: pain – exquisite and non-stop pain. I had developed some outrageously big blisters on the soles of my feet, which reminded me of their presence with every step. I needed to swap shoes again and decided to wear my trekking sandals with socks for added cushioning. I was way past caring about my appearance or indeed fashion. I did have to chuckle to myself, being German, the "socks in sandals" combination should have come naturally to me, right?

Whilst pushing my painful, now socked, feet into sandals and rummaging in my bag on the side of the road, a car stopped and a couple of rough looking guys shouted: "are you ok Miss, do you need help?" Startled, I jumped up, looked at them and was quick to say "no thank you". Glad that they promptly drove off, I couldn't help but think if I had accepted help from those two ruffians, I might not have been "ok". I immediately felt guilty about judging books by their covers. After all, it was nice of them to ask.

By now I was pretty much in the middle of nowhere, a few miles before Key West and close to the US Army Naval station. This was probably the least attractive day in ways of scenery and wildlife. It was a pretty barren area with some stretches lined by mangroves. I was mostly walking by the side of US1, which started to get a lot busier with traffic in this area. It certainly began to feel like I was walking into a city with all the traffic and noise. I missed the tranquility of Sugarloaf Key and could not help but wish myself back there.

As I got into the outskirts of Key West, the pain coming from my feet was now quite unbearable. Reaching Mile Marker 3, with only three miles to go, I suddenly could not walk another step. Not another single step! I was ready to give up, crying of pain and exhaustion and probably dehydration too. I practically collapsed into a little fast food place that happened to be by the side of the road. I just managed to order a cold drink, hobbling down the aisle and collapsing into a chair. People stared at me. Looking down at myself, I suddenly realized I must have been a sight to behold. I looked like an escapee from an institution, and not one for sane people. I was dirty, sweaty, crazy-haired and sporting the "coffee stains and socks in sandals" look I had acquired earlier that day. On top of that I had been sobbing. I quickly pulled myself together for fear of getting any more unwanted attention, or risk ending up in a straight jacket and padded room.

After a while, I felt a little better and looked at my iPad. I saw all the uplifting messages on my Facebook blog and thought to myself that there is no way I could disappoint everybody and myself. I could not simply give up three measly miles before Mile 0. I was going to make it even if it meant crawling the last three miles on all fours. However, the pain was disconcerting and I was limping badly. I needed to make sure there was nothing untoward and went to the bathroom to have a look at my feet, hoping there would be no bleeding. I felt so relieved when I took off the band-aids and saw only some very large blisters and some broken raw skin, but no blood or infection. Good news!

I bandaged up my feet once again, left the fast food joint and started limping the last three miles through gritted teeth. I was feeling every single step. This last stretch took me at least two hours to finish, having never walked so slowly in my entire life. I was a wreck. Just before getting to Mile Marker 0, I had to stop at a pharmacy to get yet more band aids and fluids. Even inside of the pharmacy store I tried to not walk around too much, everything hurt.

When I finally made it to Mile Marker 0, I was ready to collapse. Some kind lady took a picture of me as I was clutching the pole with the sign "Mile Marker 0". I was also still holding the plastic bag from the pharmacy. Being so exhausted, and beside myself, I didn't even think to take the plastic bag with band-aids out of my hands for the photo. I was mentally and physically so very drained, I believe if someone had asked me for my name, I would not have been able to tell them.

Finally, the realization sunk in: I MADE IT.

I didn't want to let go of that pole telling me I had reached Mile Marker 0 and the "End of US1". I had walked The Florida Keys all the way to the end of the famous US1. This most amazing road, 2377 miles long, stretching all the way from Fort Kent in Maine at the Canadian border, south to Key West in The Florida Keys. Here I was, at Mile Marker 0, having walked the last 105 miles of this road.

I felt like collapsing and crying with mixed feelings and so much exhaustion. On one hand, I had a huge feeling of achievement and pride, having lifted myself out of weeks of depression and negativity and managing to succeed with this walk that was planned on a whim. I had gained new strength, put my problems into perspective and felt like this achievement would give me the energy to positively plan my future. I did end the walk with the feeling that I was no longer "stuck" and able to achieve anything I wanted.

On the other hand, I also felt heavy hearted with a distinct pang of loneliness at Mile Marker 0. There was nobody to celebrate with. Not a soul. I saw people walk past me and I just blended into the general landscape, so it seemed. MoP (Man of the Past) was at home busily feeding another woman's pussy instead of welcoming me here, and I was feeling angry. I briefly thought how I had imagined arriving at Mile Marker 0 and being celebrated. In the end, there was nobody to hug me and scoop me up to a lovely hotel, so I could finally suck on a well-deserved umbrella drink and recount some stories.

It was sad to me that now I had to pick myself up yet again all alone to find my way to my humble overnight accommodation. I briefly considered hailing a taxi but there were none around. I needed a few minutes to compose myself before I could walk on - yet another mile to my lodgings. Hobbling and limping to a hostel from here felt like a complete anti-climax. This certainly was not how these stories end in the movies. Where was my happy ending? Little did I know that my adventure was very far from being over...

A Little Excursion Into Key West's History

Key West was not always a tourist town or indeed the small and quirky party town we know today. A hundred and fifty years ago, Key West had quite a different reputation and was in fact the biggest city in Florida.

By the middle of the 19th century, around 1860, wrecking had made Key West the largest and richest city in Florida. Many of the town's inhabitants' main occupation was salvaging shipwrecks from nearby reefs. The waters surrounding Key West can be treacherous to navigate, even today with our modern navigation aides, and were certainly tricky back in the day. On average, one ship per week would run aground near Key West. Then the race would begin to be the first to get to the ship, as the first man to reach the wreck would be declared "wrecking master" and was in charge of organizing the efforts. The wrecking master would receive a larger share of the prize (www.keywestshipwreck.com).

Somewhat comically, Key West in those days had a reputation for an unusually high concentration of fine furniture and chandeliers in local households. Of course all this luxury came mainly from wrecks. I even overheard a story of how at one time everybody who was anybody in Key West was learning to play the piano – after a ship with a cargo full of pianos ran aground. I don't know if this story is true, but it certainly could be.

The livelihood of Key West inhabitants was on the line in the later 19th century, when wrecking and salt declined as industries. Luckily, at the end of the 19ᵗʰ century, Key West had gained the cigar-making industry, providing much needed employment and revenue for the area.

What about the Conch Republic?

In recent times, when in Key West, you will hear about the "Conch Republic" a lot. You might even get introduced to a local "Mr. so and so", who is "a Conch". Residents born in Key West are referred to as "Conchs". When you have lived in Key West for more than seven years, you can apparently refer to yourself as a "freshwater Conch" so I understand, but in fact I have never heard it said. The origin of naming people Conchs came from an earlier settlement of Key West by Bahamians. Those Bahamians were originally called Conchs. The name stuck and is now used for anybody born in Key West.

It is only fitting, therefore, that in 1982 the city of Key West briefly declared its independence as the "Conch Republic". This humorous episode of recent island history originated in a serious protest over a blockade by the United States Border Patrol. The resulting traffic chaos angered many Key West citizens. The blockade was set up on U.S. 1, where the northern end of the Overseas Highway meets the mainland at Florida City. A traffic jam of seventeen miles ensued while US Border Patrol stopped every single car leaving The Keys, supposedly searching for illegal immigrants attempting to enter the mainland United States.

The blockade caused a crippling traffic chaos for The Keys, which of course rely heavily on the tourism industry. When the city council's complaints went unanswered by the federal government, and attempts to get an injunction against the roadblock failed in court, Mayor Wardlow and the council declared Key West's independence on April 23, 1982. In the eyes of the council, since the federal government had set up the equivalent of a border station as if they were a foreign nation, they might as well become a foreign nation. The nation took the name of "Conch Republic". As part of the protest, Mayor Wardlow was proclaimed Prime Minister of the Republic, and immediately declared war against the U.S. by symbolically breaking a loaf of stale Cuban bread over the head of a man dressed in a naval uniform. Then, there was a very quick surrender after one minute, to the man in uniform, and the new republic under Mayor Wardlow applied for one billion dollars in foreign aid. Brilliant.

Of course they didn't get aid or independence, nor did they expect to, but it was a pretty impressive and clever stunt, which

112

didn't fail to draw attention to The Florida Keys, as well as embarrassing a heavy-handed homeland security. The generated publicity for The Keys resulted in the roadblock being removed soon afterwards.

Key West inhabitants soon made good use of their publicity stunt and began to print flags, T-shirts and other souvenir merchandise bearing a "Conch Republic" logo. Incidentally, one can still find those souvenirs now, and the Conch Republic Independence Celebration is still held every April 23.

22. Arrival And "End Of Walk" Celebration In Key West

Finally, after another excruciating mile or so, I made it to my lodgings, a tiny and dark room at the Key West Hostel. I was really disappointed now. Seemingly, my head had now grown so big by achieving my goal, that I felt a 5 star hotel was in order and not what seemed like a dark roach pit (disclaimer: I did not see any "Florida pets" in the room, thankfully.). Alas, I had no money to spare for frivolities. Key West is not cheap when it comes to accommodation. I sat down on the bed and wondered whether any cockroaches would crawl over my beaten-up body that night. With a big sigh I limped into the shower.

After yet another foot-bandaging fest and making the decision to stay another night, I needed to get something to eat. Having arrived in Key West rather late in the day with not much time to explore and my feet in a sorry state, I decided that staying an extra night would be my little reward. I walked past a couple of hotels and asked if they had rooms for the next day, but prices were way out of my reach.

Almost defeated, I was drawn in by a historic house front - an old cigar factory. Inside, I started chatting to the most wonderful front desk lady, who subsequently gave me a great room rate for a little cozy attic room. After some more minutes of talking and me asking for "local" places with character to eat, she gave me a few recommendations. Off I went, with my instructions and newly found energy, knowing I would stay in a historic house the next day. I was happy. A little frivolity was indeed very good for the soul and after all, great achievements have to be celebrated in style.

I limped on to the closest of the recommended eateries, Camille's Restaurant, a place decorated in pink, pink, and more pink (think 1950s). Whilst sitting outside waiting for it to open, I slumped into one of their Adirondack chairs. I wonder whether you ever noticed that commonly, these chairs have little gaps in-between the wooden slats. No? Neither had I. I had never paid attention to it, until this evening. Those gaps conveniently provide access to an area for mosquito attack. Specifically, the area of attack is the part of your body you wish no mosquito would ever sit on, let alone sting. Apparently, Keys mosquitos have no problem stinging through two layers of clothing to reach that part of the body one sits on. Having no shame, those mosquitos were intent on adding insult to injury.

At the time, I was blissfully unaware of the feeding frenzy that was taking place in my nether regions. However, as soon as I sat down inside of the restaurant I felt an ominous itching "down there". Instead of scratching, which I thought to be inappropriate in a restaurant, I decided on ordering a "Key Lime Martini". I would have loved to sit in something cool and soothing but failing that, drinking something cool and soothing would suffice. The well-earned Martini, when it eventually arrived (remember: island time), was absolutely delicious. After indulging in a lovely plate of my favorite fish, grouper, I pulled out my trusty iPad to post the news: "I made it, having a Key Lime Martini, life is good and: thank you everybody for all your support".

As I was pondering on how relaxing this evening turned out to be, and how happy I was about my achievement, my short lived peace was rudely interrupted by hollering and noise. Down the drain went the relaxation. I looked up from my iPad somewhat irritated, to find three young guys walking into Camille's. Two had stick-on "Movember" moustaches, and the third looked like the typical good boy. He seemed to be mildly sober, keeping track of the rest of the gang. As the three of them tried to find a table, they managed to bump into every single piece of furniture in their path. People started to look up and shake heads.

After a few minutes they noticed me, of course being the only female alone in the whole restaurant, I was a prime target. Exhausted, bandaged up and with crazy hair, nevertheless I must have looked like a supermodel through their beer goggles, considering what was about to happen. I could not help but chuckle at the fact that their "single woman radar" still worked perfectly fine even though they were clearly somewhat intoxicated. They had obviously been drinking all day long. I noticed the boys trying to whisper, but their "whispering" was turned up to full volume and could clearly be heard throughout the entire restaurant and probably beyond.

The two moustached trouble makers started egging on the good boy and I was pretty sure this was about me: "Do you think she has a boyfriend? She is all alone. Are you going to talk to her? Yeah, go and ask her to join us. Wait a while, maybe the big butch boyfriend is in the restroom, ha ha." I heard everything and thought it prudent to ask for my check. My grand plan was to sprint-limp out of there in world record time, leaving just a dust cloud. They wouldn't even notice. Unfortunately, I had forgotten: it was Key West after all. Where was my check? Had they run out of paper for the print-out? Was the register not working? Did they need time to purchase a new register? And install it? What the heck was taking so long? I tried to stay calm and wished island time for once would hurry up. No such luck.

Eventually, the mildly sober guy without moustache nervously walked up to my table. He asked me politely to join their table. I declined, saying that I had just asked for the check and would be on my way out of Camille's shortly. Without much ado he went back to his table and his moustached friends. I felt a brief wave of relief. Then I heard them "whisper" again at the top of their lungs: "Try again. Ask her again. Come on." Sure enough he got up again. I saw my check coming, breathed a sigh of relief and practically ripped it out of the poor waitress's hand with a high pitched "thank you SO much".

Meanwhile, the good boy had sneaked up on me and I heard his voice: "So, where are you from?" Getting caught off guard and shuddering, I replied that I lived in Fort Lauderdale. Well, there was a lot of hurrah when he worked out that we were in fact neighbors, living next door to each other. Now, all resistance was futile and I decided to join them. It couldn't hurt for one drink, could it? My fate for the rest of the night was sealed.

Just a couple of old-fashioneds later, I was limping down Key West's most popular street, Duval, without any care in the world and with three young men. They clearly believed I was the most exotic, crazy woman they had ever met: A girl, walking The Florida Keys, all by herself? I can't remember just how many times they asked that question. They couldn't quite believe it, and I felt duly celebrated and admired. Heck, instead of the one guy that I was supposed to meet here and never showed up, I had three guys celebrating me. It was all about me and I was perking up considerably. Admittedly, the old-fashioneds had helped somewhat.

I soon found out my three boys were on a bachelor outing, naturally, and as we walked down Duval Street they received a phone-call from the groom-to-be. I could make out that he was asking them in a harsh tone where "the f*ck" they were, and whether they could make their way to "Bare Assets ASAP". Bare Assets? Something dawned on me, only to be confirmed when I pulled out my iPad with trepidation and googled "Bare Assets, Key West". Nomen est omen – this phrase is pretty much all I remember from studying Latin for seven years but it occasionally came in handy. The name, Bare Assets, had indeed been a give-away.

Upon me raising an eyebrow and saying I should head back to my room, all three of them solemnly declared with straight faces that they were "not really into strip clubs, but hey" and "when in Rome". They asked me several times to join them. I could be their Mascot, they said. All three of them promised it would all be above board and they would make sure I got back to my lodgings safely whenever I wanted to leave. Oh well, when in Key West...

At this point, of course I should have just gone to bed, but I was up for finishing my week on a high note and was feeling crazy enough to say "ok then, off to Bare Assets". Before I had time to reflect on my decision we were all sitting in Rickshaws on the way to Bare Assets which is, incidentally, the southernmost strip-club in the United States. I love to learn about geography and was about to see some interesting twin peaks and other sights.

On arrival I was introduced to all the other boys in the bachelor party group as "the girl who walked The Keys" and had to answer all kinds of questions. I didn't stop talking for about an hour. Some questions had nothing to do with my walk yet were valid. One lady at the bar said: "Can you explain to me how you got to be the only woman in a bachelor party in our club?" I couldn't really answer that one, other than explaining to her that it just kind of happened.

The evening turned out quite amusing, with the boys vying for my attention. I had a whale of a time, they were well educated and fun to be with. Then, the evening took a turn for the worse as one of the stripper took my hand and led me into a cubicle with one of the young men, the one I had been talking to most. He was a dashingly handsome young surgeon. When I lamely protested, she was surprised: "What, this is not your boyfriend?" She tried to get me to dance, but I was somehow distracted by the fact that her "bare assets" threatened to poke my eyes out. I simply had to touch them to find out whether they were as buoyant as they looked.

Unfortunately, asking if I could touch them clearly gave her the wrong impression. I was now fair game, in her eyes. A few seconds later, the stripper swiftly and in one exact movement yanked down the top of my dress. In disbelief, I froze until I felt an uncanny draft of cold air on my right breast, which – much to my horror – was now ever so un-elegantly exposed. Worse, the exposed breast happened to be pointing exactly at the (sitting) guy's eyes, as if to introduce itself: "Well, hello, young man!"

As the girl started to encourage the guy to do something with my exposed right breast, he and I exchanged looks of horror and embarrassment, which should never be exchanged between two almost strangers. He did not move. Suddenly, I was stone-cold sober, and the dashingly handsome surgeon was looking less dashing and increasingly pale. He seemed completely glued to his seat. In fact, I was not sure he was still breathing.

This whole scene did not last longer than a couple of seconds before my brain instructed my hand to pull up my dress at the speed of light. My dignity was intact again. Suddenly, my curiosity of strip-clubs, augmented breasts and what bachelor parties do, was totally and irrevocably quenched for the night, possibly for life. The stripper, meanwhile, seemed totally oblivious and was intent on breathing life into the somewhat lifeless doctor. Turning towards me, she said: "Kiss my neck."

I was out of there. Kiss her neck? Me? Touching an augmented breast out of curiosity once in one's life was ok in my opinion. However, having one's dress pulled down in front of a virtual stranger, who looked like he was about to have a cardiac arrest, and then being asked to kiss the neck of a girl? That was definitely my cue to leave. The celebration of my walk was coming to an abrupt end.

It was time for me to get out of Bare Assets promptly and get my own assets safely to bed. Thankfully, one of the guys said he would take me home with a detour via their, quite luxurious, hotel and a nightcap. Yes, yes, I know, how naïve of me. I wanted to see their apartment as it was in a beautiful complex and there were plenty of people around, so it felt reasonably safe (disclaimer: don't do this!). I also seriously thought we would – after a civilized nightcap – walk to my hostel. He, however, being a somewhat intoxicated young man, who had just collected a large dose of "horny" at a strip club, had of course other plans. I didn't notice until we were halfway through our nightcap, when he simply dropped his pants (all of them), saying he "wouldn't mind a bit of action".

Oh dear. There it was again, my cue to leave! I froze for a moment, before running out of there as fast as possible. Grabbing my bag, I mumbled "thanks and bye", and all I heard was the front door dropping into the latch. Click. I briefly wondered for how long he stood there in all his glory. I would never know. Before drawing a second breath I was already out on the street. Phew.

When I got to my little room, only a few minutes later, I collapsed on the bed and could not stop laughing. Here I was, after having made it all the way from Mile Marker 105 to Mile 0 and on to the southernmost strip club. My trip ended with nothing less than my own personal male stripper. It had been quite the eye-opening journey in many respects.

23. A Deserved Vacation Day In Key West

My headache and I got up quite early. I checked myself and the backpack for any critters we might have collected at this abode, hastily collected my belongings and hurried to the old cigar factory hotel as fast as I could. Why? I had seen their delicious breakfast menu the day before. My day started with well-deserved eggs benedict and plenty of coffee. After having skipped breakfast and coffee for most of the week, this felt like heaven. Just what the doctor ordered. Finally, civilization had me back and it felt great.

After the hearty breakfast, I set off to spend the day enjoying beautiful Key West.

Starting off with a little stroll through Duval Street, I checked out all the colorful little stores and bars. After the walk, my feet begged for mercy on account of having been bashed for a whole week and I decided to let them get some well deserved rest and hopped on the Conch Train. Much to my surprise – I had expected this to be touristy nonsense – it was a great little informative trip around Key West. Plenty of photo opportunities without having to take a single step, it felt like heaven and if my feet could have talked, no doubt they'd have thanked me profusely.

I only had this one free day after my walk and as you can imagine, my intent at the end of a day of sightseeing was this: celebrating my achievement and having fun. I did not want to miss out on a celebration just because I was alone. In fact, one good thing I learnt during that year and especially during the walk: love and celebrate yourself. Self-love means doing things that bring joy, whether those are little things such as a thirty minute walk in nature, or big ones such as a vacation overseas.

I set off to do just that: celebrate myself. Having been told about the famous Mallory Square sunset celebration, I decided to head straight there. Every day, around two hours before sunset, Mallory Square is transformed into an open-air show space for street performers, arts and craft exhibitors and food trucks. All this takes place behind the breathtaking backdrop of the sun setting over the

Gulf of Mexico. What's not to like? I loved it. After getting a Mojito from a little stand and a few conch fritters from another, I watched the Cat Man show off his trained cats. Although he had me nearly choking on the fritters with sentences like: "don't play with my pussy."

Having satisfied all my desires for the day, I set off for a stroll back to my lovely historic cigar factory. I did not get too far when I was asked by a couple of men whether I wanted to blow their conchs. Huh? I thought this was some kind of indecent proposal, but lo and behold as I declined and walked on, I could indeed hear them blowing into conch shells. Key West is definitely one of a kind.

Not quite ready for bed yet, I went for a little nightcap in the lovely garden bar of my hotel. Apparently, the day had yet another surprise in store for me. Sitting at a table by myself, some people came up to me to chat and I was introduced to a German girl. Being quite the introvert, I didn't really want to talk or interact too much and was intent on finishing my cocktail and going to bed. However, once we got chatting and the girl started telling me where she grew up, my jaw dropped. It was the very little town I was born in! You can imagine the excitement, as we found out we attended the same school for some years and even had some common friends. What a small world it is.

For me, it was an unexpected and magical ending to a challenging but wonderful week. It also goes to show that you never know what or whom you will find when you embark on a little adventure, be it new friends or old.

Chapter 5

The Key West Experience In A Nutshell

I could not finish a book on walking The Florida Keys without at least giving a few pointers of things to do in Key West, most of which I have enjoyed myself. If time is limited, my suggestions let you capture the essence of crazy, cute and historical Key West in a day. If time is not limited, the sky is your limit, as there are probably 365 or more things you could do in and around Key West.

24. What Is There To Do In Key West?

Bars, Bars And More Bars.

Let's start with the obvious first: Bars, bars, bars!

The first thing you will notice: there are bars everywhere in Key West. If I tried to give you a "best bars in Key West" write-up, it would turn into a whole book. Bars are pretty much a way of life down there, and yes, you will see people in them from early in the day. Tee-totals beware, this is scary stuff. You will try to navigate the sidewalk with all the jolly characters from Key West, tourists from the whole world and the obligatory bachelor and bachelorette parties. Therefore, Key West is easier to tolerate when you have had a few cocktails and left the car at the hotel. Most places in and around Duval Street are walkable, and why not walk off the cocktail calories?

I couldn't get away without mentioning some of the more interesting and historic bars, of which there are plenty.

First, obviously, we have to talk about Sloppy Joe's. Nobody should ever visit Key West without stopping at least for a drink here, even if it is a soda. Sloppy Joe's opened its doors, albeit under a different name, on the very day Prohibition ended on 5th December 1933. Clearly, they did not waste a moment. Of course, we all know Sloppy Joe's as one of Ernest Hemingway's favorite hang-outs in Key West. Hemingway was a long time friend of the owner, Joe Russell, who had not only been supplying Hemingway with his Scotch during Prohibition, but also been his fishing partner and boat captain (www.sloppyjoes.com). I love Sloppy Joes, for the reason that throughout the years it has remained largely unchanged. If you happen to be there at the Hemingway look-alike contest held every July, you have to attend and cast your vote.

There are plenty of other historic bars worth noting, for example Captain Tony's Saloon, opposite Sloppy Joe's, and in fact situated in the original building of the first Sloppy Joe's (it later moved into the building across the street). Captain Tony's Saloon opened in 1958 in this historic building that had previously served the city as an ice house and morgue before it changed to a bar in 1933. The grisliness doesn't stop there, however, as this is also the site of the famous hanging tree of Key West. The tree is said to have been the place of hanging of sixteen pirates as well as one woman who stabbed her husband and children to death. The tree has seen as many as seventy five hangings altogether. It is a huge tree and still there with the bar. If you want to have a drink in a museum with a sordid history, head there. Incidentally, as Captain Tony's Saloon was originally opened in 1933, this is indeed the oldest bar site in Key West - in the 20th century at least (www.capttonyssaloon.com).

There is also the Green Parrot and The Brown Derby Bar, a favorite hang-out for sailors. Both of these bars originate roughly in the same period as Sloppy Joe's and Captain Tony's Saloon, and are still going strong today. As mentioned before: there are plenty of bars in Key West. By all means go on a little bar excursion. Although there is of course so much more to Key West than just the bars.

Historic Properties

There are many fine historic houses which, although Key West has seen plenty of brushes with (and hits from) tropical thunderstorms and hurricanes during the last 150 years, remain relatively unscathed. Indeed, most have been lovingly renovated.

You can of course read up on all the architectural styles to see in Key West. Then, you may marvel at your new-found knowledge and look at all the different style houses in the "Old Town" historic district. According to the Florida Department of State, Division of Historical Resources, the Key West Historic District contains almost 2500 historic houses and structures (www.dosmyflorida.com).

Alternatively, if you have just walked 105 miles and have sore feet like I had, and no intentions of hitting the library in gorgeous weather, my recommendation is to hop on the Conch Train. There, you get the historic facts in easily digestible form, while you relax on a cute open-air train trolley and have someone drive you around. I usually avoid the overly touristy areas and attractions but this is an exceptional tour. The Conch Train offers just the right mix of fun and education, as well as being very convenient.

If you only have a day to spend in lovely Key West, this little itinerary combined with a little walk around Duval Street may be all you really want to do and have time for. Additionally, I would certainly recommend seeing the sunset celebration at Mallory Square, which I describe in detail below.

On The Water

If you have been wise enough to include a couple more days stay in Key West, then the sky (and the ocean) is literally your limit. Where do I start? Since I mentioned the sky first, how about paragliding or parasailing in Key West? For ocean lovers, there are so many options, such as boating, kayaking and snorkel trips out to the reefs, for example. Perhaps the most unusual of ocean adventures deserves a mention: Dry Tortugas National Park.

Dry Tortugas National Park is a remote cluster of little islands about seventy miles from Key West, location of the magnificent Fort Jefferson and to date the largest masonry structure in the western

Hemisphere. The Dry Tortugas are not just a great destination for those interested in history, but they are also teeming with sea life and make for an amazing diving and snorkeling excursion. If you are brave enough, you can even pitch a tent here overnight. Just remember to bring everything you need including your own drinking water. In case you haven't already guessed, the islands were named the "dry" Tortugas because there is no fresh water to be found here. The name Dry Tortugas was given to the islands to warn sailors of the lack of fresh water, and inform them of an abundance of turtles ("Tortugas" means "Sea Turtles" in Spanish), an important food source back in the day.

The Dry Tortugas trip takes up a whole day with a ferry leaving from Key West (Yankee Clipper). You could do the trip in half a day with a sea plane, if you are so inclined. If you do not have so much time, there are plenty of other ways to get on the water, for example sunset cruises and various boat tours, which can take you snorkeling and diving for a few hours.

Museums And Aquariums

On land, there are plenty of options, starting with many interesting and quirky museums to visit. A must-see is Ernest Hemingway's house, which is beautiful and has quite a few descendants of Hemingway's famous six-toed cats as residents.

How about Truman's Little White House? This is now a charming and interesting little museum that has a long history, including a spell as Harry S. Truman's winter retreat. There is also the famous Mel Fishers Maritime Museum, which displays an array of artifacts that were found on sunken ships around Key West (oh those deadly reefs!). The Shipwreck Museum also showcases Key West's history as a wrecking town with dressed-up museum assistants doing a great job of bringing history to life.

For those more interested in aquariums there are also options, for example the free Florida Keys Eco Discovery Center. It boasts plenty of interactive displays ideal for kids, as well as a 2500 gallon reef tank with living corals and tropical fish.

The list of things to do in Key West is almost endless and this is intended to offer just a little taster and is not an exhaustive resource by any means.

Mallory Square Sunset Celebration – To End A Perfect Day

The Mallory Square sunset celebration is a total must see for anyone visiting Key West. It combines many of the wonderful things Key West has to offer, such as great food and drink, street entertainer fun and usually (weather permitting) throws in a stunning sunset over the Gulf of Mexico. Everybody who visits Key West should see the Mallory Square celebration at least once.

The street performers are excellent, with "Cat Man" undoubtedly the biggest attraction. Cat Man has been saying "don't play with my pussy" with a hilarious French accent for over thirty years. He trains cats (yes you heard right) to do all kinds of little tricks, including jumping through hoops, even fiery ones. Sometimes – cats being cats – they refuse, but not to worry. Cat Man, being a true professional, has incorporated various cat tantrums into his show. Fact is, anyone who manages to make a cat jump through a hoop of fire is an incredible magician.

After you have recovered from seeing trained cats, something you thought you would never see, it will be time for a cocktail. Head to the Mojito stand outside of the Westin Hotel, conveniently located right next to Cat Man's usual location. Mojito Man is not the youngest, but I do hope he will carry on for many years, because his Mojitos are extremely delicious. I understand he has been the Key West champion Mojito maker for the last few years and if you are lucky enough to catch him, it is worth a little wait in line. Actually, it is worth a long wait in line. As well as Mojito man, there is also a food truck with conch fritters in the vicinity, conveniently located close to the Mojitos. Do I need to say more?

Once again, the list of things to do in Key West is well beyond the scope of this little book. I intended to offer just a little snapshot of what I enjoyed the most, and it is not an exhaustive resource or list of "things to do". I recommend a quick visit to the Tourist Information on the first day of your stay, or the last day of your walk if you dare to follow in my footsteps, and you will be totally overwhelmed by all the amazing things that Key West and its surroundings can offer you. Why not stay a week or two?

CHAPTER 6

Was The Walk "Worth It"?

I understand that you might want to ask: was this walk worth the sore feet, cost and time investment? Did all this make a real and lasting impact on my life? Can something similar make an impact on your life?

After all, this was just a week long walk and compared to a hike across the United States (yes, people do that), a pretty modest challenge. As such, it would perhaps be too much to expect this walk to make a big change in anyone's life. Of course, I just went back home and carried on as before. Just not quite.

25. The Benefits Of Completing A Multi-Day Walk Of The Florida Keys

We must never underestimate the power of stepping outside our comfort zone, no matter how brief. No, this was not a several month long trip across the Appalachian Mountain Trail or across the United States. No, I was not fighting bears or eating berries I had to pick myself and having to drink water from springs along the way. No, I was not "roughing it" and had a nice soft bed to sleep in every night. I spent most evenings in relative comfort with a decent meal and a nice cold drink or two.

However, walking through one's own personal pain barrier yet carrying on despite discomfort and pain, is an experience that can change one's mindset considerably. Achieving a set goal, such as walking over one hundred miles on a tight schedule and completing the challenge, can lay the foundation for future goal setting and success, whether in private life or in one's career.

In my case, achieving my goal of walking The Florida Keys to Mile Marker 0 gave me new hope that I could turn my life around. In many ways, it was a healing and growing experience. My mind was recalibrated from dwelling on negativity to seeing possibilities and thinking more positively. In many ways, the walk gave me a new lease of life and had me feel like I could conquer any difficulty. Instead of problems and setbacks, I finally saw opportunities for shaping my own future. Having to leave and planning out a new life in Europe suddenly didn't seem like such a big deal anymore.

The walk also gave me more self-esteem and confidence for facing difficult situations. Further, being an introvert and having to speak to strangers for a whole week, as well as having to adjust to a new environment every day, pushed me out of my personal comfort zone. Last but not least, finishing the walk successfully brought me a lot of joy and happiness.

There is also the very important aspect of nourishing the soul, which is important at any time but especially so in a difficult phase of one's life. My soul was amply fed by the wonderful wildlife I saw, the lovely people I met, the unplanned celebration I had at the end of my walk and meeting a dear new old friend. I will never forget any of it. The memories of this week will last a lifetime and will always provide something to think back on fondly. I would not want to miss any of it.

Would I recommend walking The Keys over other routes?

Absolutely! It is not a very daunting route or time frame and doable by reasonably fit persons of most ages. Of course, one has to be mindful of a number of factors such as the heat and wear and tear on one's body. However, all risk factors can be minimized by good preparation and planning, as well as embarking on the walk in cooler months. Preparation is certainly the key to walking The Keys.

I would want to encourage anyone who contemplates anything like this and anywhere in the world, to just go and do it. Doing something a little crazy, as long as it is done with rational planning and preparation will add spice, excitement and a sense of achievement to anybody's life.

It's a case of feeling a little fear and doing it anyway. Most of all, don't let anyone discourage you. I too had some people telling me it was too dangerous, too tough and too "crazy" to walk The Florida Keys alone as a single woman. Although of course those people meant well, I am forever glad not to have listened to them.

It helped me in the planning stage to become aware of many people who have successfully completed much more gruesome and difficult challenges than walking the beautiful Florida Keys. The morale is: Get out of your comfort zone and you will be amazed at what you can achieve.

Acknowledgements

A big thank you to all my local friends. I could not have done it without your encouragement. I also thank all those who supported me daily, via social media, spurning me on when I felt exhausted and in pain. I probably couldn't have done it without the support.

Thank you to Gary Smailes of Bubblecow for editing my manuscript, and to Adisa Zahirović for the beautiful cover design. Thank you also to eagle-eyed Karen D'Uva for reading the proof.

A big thank you to Edgewater Lodge, Daniela Gonzales and Cynthia. Fond memories!

A huge thank you to my wonderful husband-to-be James Armstrong and his unfailing moral (and IT) support. He also makes the best Magaritas outside of Mexico, which helps.

Thank you also to my readers. I hope this little book will give you some inspiration.

Lastly, this book is not a work of fiction. Everything contained herein happened to the best of my memory. I have, where appropriate, changed the names in the book to maintain privacy.

Life indeed does write the best stories.

References And Further Reading

Bramson, Seth H.: *Speedway To Sunshine: The Story Of The Florida East Coast Railway*. Ontario: Boston Mills Press, 2003.

Bratman, Gregory N., et al: "Nature experience reduces rumination and subgenual prefrontal cortex activation",
Proceedings of the National Academy of Sciences of the United States of America Vol 112, no.28.

Hemingway, Ernest: "Who Murdered The Vets" , *The New Masses* (17th Sept. 1935).

Kraus Whitbourne, Susan: "Get Out And Walk! Your Brain Will Thank You", *Psychology Today* (15th Feb.2011)

Montgomery, Ben: *Grandma Gatewood's Walk: The Inspiring Story Of The Woman Who Saved The Appalachian Trail*. Chicago: Chicago Review Press, 2014.

Parks, Pat: *The Railroad That Died At Sea*. Key West: Langley Press, 1968.

Website References

www.walkingthekeys.com

www.tamarascharf.com

www.heart.org

www.quickfacts.census.gov/qfd/

www.koeppen-geiger.vu-wien.ac.at

www.floridastateparks.org/trail/FloridaKeys

www.keyshistory.org

www.friendsofoldseven.org

www.v-e-n-u-e.com/The-Bat-Tower

www.keywestshipwreck.com

www.sloppyjoes.com

www.capttonyssaloon.com

www.dosmyflorida.com

http://www.fla-keys.com

Made in United States
North Haven, CT
19 January 2022

14969318R00085